SCIENTIFIC WRITING AND RESEARCH QUALITY

ENV BOOKS SERIES

SCIENTIFIC WRITING AND RESEARCH QUALITY

Editors

Dr. Prasann Kumar

Division of Research and Development
Lovely Professional University
Jalandhar - 144 411 (Punjab)
(India)

&

Dr. Pawan Kumar 'Bharti'

Society for Environment, Health Awareness of
Nutrition & Toxicology (SEHAT)
B-225/5D, Top Floor, Subhash Gali, Road No. 7, Block B
Ashok Nagar, Shahdara, Delhi - 110 093
(India)

DPH

DISCOVERY PUBLISHING HOUSE PVT. LTD.
INDIA

Published by:
Namit Wasan
DISCOVERY PUBLISHING HOUSE PVT. LTD.
4383/4B, Ansari Road, Darya Ganj
New Delhi-110 002 (India)
Phone : +91-11-23279245; 23253475; 43596065
E-mail : discoverybooksindia@gmail.com
discoverypublishinghouse@gmail.com
namitwasan9@gmail.com
web : www.discoverypublishinggroup.com

First Edition: **2020**

ISBN: 978-93-88854-48-1

Scientific Writing and Research Quality

Printed at:
Infinity Imaging Systems
Delhi

PREFACE

Writing is a very important part of science; it is used to document and communicate ideas, activities and findings to others. Scientific writing can take many forms from a lab notebook to a project report, or from a paper in an academic journal to an article in a scientific magazine.

To reflect the characteristics of good scientific writing in your own work, you need to think about the way that you write and the language that you use. A good scientific author will have given consideration to the following choices in writing, making decisions that improve the effectiveness of the writing. To make your writing clear, accurate and concise you should consider carefully the words that you use, and the ways in which you use them. In most scientific writing you will need to use some scientific or technical terms in order to be clear and unambiguous. However, use such terms only when you need to do so and do not try to impress the reader by using unnecessary technical jargon or lengthy words. Abbreviations can be a very useful way of saving time and avoiding repetition, but they can be confusing and might not be understood by everyone. Use standard abbreviations where these exist, and reduce your use of abbreviations to an absolute minimum; they are rarely essential.

The present book updates the subject content of Quality Writing of Research Article; Research Design; Topic for Research Work in Agriculture; Effective Report writing in Science; Concept of 3Is for effective research; writing a winning grant proposal; Intellectual property rights; Plagiarism in research; Research towards research excellence in research; Microarrys: insight for research; Research progress and its understanding.

Thanks are due to publisher and contributors from various institutions and universities.

The book will be helpful for the researchers, academia working in the field of Quality Writing; Research Design; Topic for Research Work in Agriculture; Effective Report writing in Science; Concept of 3Is; writing a grant proposal; Intellectual property rights; Plagiarism; Research towards research excellence in research; Microarrys; and research progress.

Editors
(envbooks@gmail.com)

CONTENTS

Scientific Writing and Research Quality
Edited by: Dr. Prasann Kumar & Dr. Pawan Kumar 'Bharti'
ISBN: 978-93-88854-48-1
Edition: 2020
Published by: Discovery Publishing House Pvt. Ltd., New Delhi (India)

1 Introduction

Writing is a very important part of science; it is used to document and communicate ideas, activities and findings to others. Scientific writing can take many forms from a lab notebook to a project report, or from a paper in an academic journal to an article in a scientific magazine. This compendium focuses on scientific writing for academic course work, much of which is devoted to describing and explaining.

Characteristics of Good Scientific Writing

Good scientific writing is:

- clear - it avoids unnecessary detail;
- simple - it uses direct language, avoiding vague or complicated sentences. Technical terms and jargon are used only when they are necessary for accuracy;
- impartial - it avoids making assumptions (Everyone knows that ...) and unproven statements (It can never be proved that ...). It presents how and where data were collected and supports its conclusions with evidence;
- structured logically - ideas and processes are expressed in a logical order. The text is divided into sections with clear headings;
- accurate - it avoids vague and ambiguous language such as about, approximately, almost;
- objective - statements and ideas are supported by appropriate evidence that demonstrates how conclusions have been drawn as well as acknowledging the work of others.

Developing Good Scientific Writing

To reflect the characteristics of good scientific writing in your own work, you need to think about the way that you write and the language that you use. A good scientific author will have given consideration to the following choices in writing, making decisions that improve the effectiveness of the writing.

Choosing the Words

To make your writing clear, accurate and concise you should consider carefully the words that you use, and the ways in which you use them.

Technical terms

In most scientific writing you will need to use some scientific or technical terms in order to be clear and unambiguous. However, use such terms only when you need to do so and do not try to impress the reader by using unnecessary technical jargon or lengthy words.

Abbreviations

Abbreviations can be a very useful way of saving time and avoiding repetition, but they can be confusing and might not be understood by everyone. Use standard abbreviations where these exist, and reduce your use of abbreviations to an absolute minimum; they are rarely essential.

Use objective rather than subjective language

Objective language is language that is impartial and states a fact or process; subjective language is open to question or interpretation as it implies personal thought or belief. For example:

Objective

The car travelled at 38 kilometres per houris a clear, objective statement of fact. However:

Subjective

The contents of the test tube turned a beautiful blue colouruses beautiful in a way that is subjective because it cannot be measured or accurately explained to the reader. Always use language that is concrete and specific rather than vague and personal.

Choosing a 'voice'

Scientific writers have a tendency to use passive rather than active expressions; stating that a was affected by b uses the passive voice while stating that b did something to a uses the active voice. The following example shows a sentence written in both the passive and active voices.

passive The experiment was designed by the research officer

active The research officer designed the experiment

The passive voice is particularly useful when:

you wish your writing to be formal and depersonalised:

passive It was agreed that the experiment should be...

active We agreed that the experiment should be...

information about the agent is obvious or unimportant:

passive Extra solvent was added to the flask

active The technician added extra solvent to the flask;

you do not know the identity of the agent:

passive The water pipe was broken in three places

active Something/someone had broken the water pipe in three places

However, the use of the passive voice can lead to clumsy and overcomplicated sentences.

passive Difficulty was experienced in obtaining the product in a high state of purity

is rather convoluted way of saying

active The product was difficult to purify

which is a much clearer and more straightforward statement.

In general, the active voice is clearer, more direct and easier to read, but the passive voice can be more appropriate in particular circumstances. What is most important is for you to be aware of how you are writing, and how the voice that you choose affects the tone and the meaning of your words.

Personal or impersonal?

Scientific writers often try to avoid the use of personal expressions or statements in order to make their writing seem more impartial and formal. The following sentence has been written with both personal and impersonal expressions to highlight the contrast between the two writing styles.

impersonal The explanation for this phenomenon may be found in…

personal We/I believe that the explanation for this phenomenon may be found in...

However, used indiscriminately, writing impersonally can result in clumsy statements through an excessive use of the passive voice. This can lead to ambiguity or inaccuracy in your written work, for example:

impersonal & passive

It was decided that the temperature should be raised gives no information about the identity of the people who made the decision.

personal & active

We decided that the temperature should be raised avoids ambiguity and makes the sentence sound more direct, but uses the personal and rather informal we.

impersonal & active

The research team decided that the temperature should be raised is clear and direct.

Think carefully about your use of impersonal and personal expressions, taking care to ensure that your writing is always clear and unambiguous.

Using tenses

Scientific writing frequently uses the past tense, particularly when the main focus of the writing is to describe experiments or observations that took place prior to the time of writing, for example:

The data were analysed.

The solution was decanted.

The temperature was recorded.

However, the past tense may not be appropriate for everything that you write and sometimes you will need to combine different tenses in the same piece of writing. For example, the use of different tenses can help to clarify what happened or what you did in the past (past tense), what you conclude (present tense) and what will be an issue for the future (future tense). The following sentences show how different tenses can be used to achieve clarity in your written work.

The experiment was carried out in a sterile environment (past tense for a statement of what happened). It is particularly important to avoid contamination (present tense for a statement that is a general 'truth'). It will be necessary to ensure that the same conditions are replicated in future experiments (future tense for a recommendation for the future).

An appropriate use of past, present and future tenses can contribute to a clear and unambiguous writing style.

Sentence Length

Sentences that are too short and poorly connected can be irritating to read. Conversely, sentences that are too long and rambling are difficult to follow and are likely to be confusing. Use a sentence length that allows your thoughts to flow clearly. As a general rule there should be no more than 20-25 words in any one sentence. You may be able to reduce your sentence length by:

cutting out unnecessary words

like might replace along the lines of

now may be just as appropriate as at the present time

we can now turn our attention to could perhaps be cut out entirely;

dividing complex sentences into separate phrases or sentences.

If a breakdown occurs it is important that alternative supplies are available and the way that this is done is for the power stations to be linked through the high voltage transmission lines so that all of them contribute to the total supply of energy and an unexpectedly large demand can be handled.

can be re-written thus:

If a breakdown occurs it is important that alternative supplies are available; this is done by linking power stations through the high voltage transmission lines. All of them thus contribute to the total supply of energy and an unexpectedly large demand can be handled.

Scientific Writing

Scientific writing is a technical form of writing that is designed to communicate scientific information to other scientists. Depending on the specific scientific genre—a journal article, a scientific poster, or a research proposal, for example—some aspects of the writing may change, such as its purpose, audience, or organization. Many aspects of scientific writing, however, varylittle across these writing genres. Important hallmarks of all scientific writing are summarized below.

What are some important hallmarks of professional scientific writing?

1. Its primary audience is other scientists. Because of its intended audience, student-oriented or general-audience details, definitions, and explanations — which are often necessary in lab manuals or reports — are not terribly useful. Explaining general-knowledge concepts or how routine procedures were performed actually tends to obstruct clarity, make the writing wordy, and detract from its professional tone.
2. It is concise and precise. A goal of scientific writing is to communicate scientific information clearly and concisely. Flowery, ambiguous, wordy, and redundant language run counter to the purpose of the writing.
3. It must be set within the context of other published work. Because science builds on and corrects itself over time, scientific writing must be situated in and reference the findings of previous work. This context serves variously as motivation for new work being proposed or the paper being written, as points of departure or congruence for new findings and interpretations, and as evidence of the authors' knowledge and expertise in the field.

All of the information under "The Essentials" tab is intended to help you to build your knowledge and skills as a scientific writer regardless of the scientific discipline you are studying or the specific assignment you might be working on. In addition to discussions of audience and purpose, professional conventions like conciseness and specificity, and how to find and use literature references appropriately, we also provide guidelines for how to organize your writing and how to avoid some common mechanical errors.

History

Scientific writing in English started in the 14th century.

The Royal Society established good practice for scientific writing. Founder member Thomas Sprat wrote on the importance of plain and accurate description rather than rhetorical flourishes in his History of the Royal Society of London. Robert Boyle emphasized the importance of not boring the reader with a dull, flat style.

Because most scientific journals accept manuscripts only in English, an entire industry has developed to help non-native English speaking authors improve their text before submission. It is just now becoming an accepted practice to utilize the benefits of these services. This is making it easier for scientists to focus on their research and still get published in top journals.

Besides the customary readability tests, software tools relying on Natural Language Processing to analyze text help writer scientists evaluate the quality of their manuscripts prior to submission to a journal. SWAN, a Java app written by researchers from the University of Eastern Finland is such a tool.

Research

Research is "creative and systematic work undertaken to increase the stock of knowledge, including knowledge of humans, culture and society, and the use of this stock of knowledge to devise new applications." It is used to establish or confirm facts, reaffirm the results of previous work, solve new or existing problems, support theorems, or develop new theories. A research project may also be an expansion on past work in the field. Research projects can be used to develop further knowledge on a topic, or in the example of a school research project, they can be used to further a student's research prowess to prepare them for future jobs or reports. To test the validity of instruments, procedures, or experiments, research may replicate elements of prior projects or the project as a whole. The primary purposes of basic research (as opposed to applied research) are documentation, discovery, interpretation, or the research and development (R&D) of methods and systems for the advancement of human knowledge. Approaches to research depend on epistemologies, which vary considerably both within and between humanities and sciences. There are several forms of research: scientific, humanities, artistic, economic, social, business, marketing, practitioner research, life, technological, etc. The scientific study of research practices is known as meta-research.

Research has been defined in a number of different ways, and while there are similarities, there does not appear to be a single, all-encompassing definition that is embraced by all who engage in it.

One definition of research is used by the OECD, "Any creative systematic activity undertaken in order to increase the stock of knowledge, including knowledge of man, culture and society, and the use of this knowledge to devise new applications."

Another definition of research is given by John W. Creswell, who states that "research is a process of steps used to collect and analyze information to increase our understanding of a topic or issue". It consists of three steps: pose a question, collect data to answer the question, and present an answer to the question.

The Merriam-Webster Online Dictionary defines research in more detail as "studious inquiry or examination; especially : investigation or experimentation aimed at the discovery and interpretation of facts, revision of accepted theories or laws in the light of new facts, or practical application of such new or revised theories or laws".

Forms of Research

Original research is research that is not exclusively based on a summary, review or synthesis of earlier publications on the subject of research. This material is of a primary source character. The purpose of the original research is to produce new knowledge, rather than to present the existing knowledge in a new form (e.g., summarized or classified).

Original research can take a number of forms, depending on the discipline it pertains to. In experimental work, it typically involves direct or indirect observation of the researched subject(s), e.g., in the laboratory or in the field, documents the methodology, results, and conclusions of an experiment or set of experiments, or offers a novel interpretation of previous results. In analytical work, there are typically some new (for example) mathematical results produced, or a new way of approaching an existing problem. In some subjects which do not typically carry out experimentation or analysis of this kind, the originality is in the particular way existing understanding is changed or re-interpreted based on the outcome of the work of the researcher.

The degree of originality of the research is among major criteria for articles to be published in academic journals and usually established by means of peer review. Graduate students are commonly required to perform original research as part of a dissertation.

Scientific research is a systematic way of gathering data and harnessing curiosity. This research provides scientific information and theories for the explanation of the nature and the properties of the world. It makes practical applications possible. Scientific research is funded by public authorities, by charitable organizations and by private groups, including many companies. Scientific research can be subdivided into different classifications according to their academic and application disciplines. Scientific research is a widely used criterion for judging the standing of an academic institution, but some argue that such is an inaccurate assessment of the institution, because the quality of research does not tell about the quality of teaching (these do not necessarily correlate).

Research in the humanities involves different methods such as for example hermeneutics and semiotics. Humanities scholars usually do not search for the ultimate correct answer to a question, but instead, explore the issues and details that surround it. Context is always important, and context can be social, historical, political, cultural, or ethnic. An example of research in the humanities is historical research, which is embodied in historical method. Historians use primary sources and other evidence to systematically investigate a topic, and then to write histories in the form of accounts of the past. Other studies aim to merely examine the occurrence of behaviours in societies and communities, without particularly looking for reasons or motivations to explain these. These studies may be qualitative or quantitative, and can use a variety of approaches, such as queer theory or feminist theory.

Artistic research, also seen as 'practice-based research', can take form when creative works are considered both the research and the object of research itself. It is the debatable body of thought which offers an alternative to purely scientific methods in research in its search for knowledge and truth.

Scientific Research

Generally, research is understood to follow a certain structural process. Though step order may vary depending on the subject matter and researcher, the following steps are usually part of most formal research, both basic and applied:

- **Observations and formation of the topic:** Consists of the subject area of one's interest and following that subject area to conduct subject related research. The subject area should not be randomly chosen since it requires reading a vast amount of literature on the topic to determine the gap in the literature the researcher intends to narrow. A keen interest in the chosen subject area is advisable. The research will have to be justified by linking its importance to already existing knowledge about the topic.
- **Hypothesis:** A testable prediction which designates the relationship between two or more variables.
- **Conceptual definition:** Description of a concept by relating it to other concepts.
- **Operational definition:** Details in regards to defining the variables and how they will be measured/assessed in the study.
- **Gathering of data:** Consists of identifying a population and selecting samples, gathering information from or about these samples by using specific research instruments. The instruments used for data collection must be valid and reliable.
- **Analysis of data:** Involves breaking down the individual pieces of data to draw conclusions about it.
- **Data Interpretation:** This can be represented through tables, figures, and pictures, and then described in words.

- Test, revising of hypothesis.
- Conclusion, reiteration if necessary.

A common misconception is that a hypothesis will be proven (see, rather, null hypothesis). Generally, a hypothesis is used to make predictions that can be tested by observing the outcome of an experiment. If the outcome is inconsistent with the hypothesis, then the hypothesis is rejected (see falsifiability). However, if the outcome is consistent with the hypothesis, the experiment is said to support the hypothesis. This careful language is used because researchers recognize that alternative hypotheses may also be consistent with the observations. In this sense, a hypothesis can never be proven, but rather only supported by surviving rounds of scientific testing and, eventually, becoming widely thought of as true.

A useful hypothesis allows prediction and within the accuracy of observation of the time, the prediction will be verified. As the accuracy of observation improves with time, the hypothesis may no longer provide an accurate prediction. In this case, a new hypothesis will arise to challenge the old, and to the extent that the new hypothesis makes more accurate predictions than the old, the new will supplant it. Researchers can also use a null hypothesis, which states no relationship or difference between the independent or dependent variables.

REFERENCE

https://www2.le.ac.uk/offices/ld/resources/writing/writing-resources/science

http://sites.middlebury.edu/middsciwriting/overview/

https://en.wikipedia.org/wiki/Scientific_writing

https://www.le.ac.uk/oerresources/ssds/writingskills/page_65.htm

https://en.wikipedia.org/wiki/Research

https://www.questionpro.com/blog/what-is-research/

Scientific Writing and Research Quality Pages 10-17
Edited by: Dr. Prasann Kumar & Dr. Pawan Kumar 'Bharti'
ISBN: 978-93-88854-48-1
Edition: 2020
Published by: Discovery Publishing House Pvt. Ltd., New Delhi (India)

2

Quality Writing of Research Article for High Impact Journals

Prasann Kumar[1,2]* & Shipa Rani Dey[1]

GRAPHICAL ABSTRACT

Keywords: *Article, Impact, Journal, Writing, Research, Paper*

Introduction

Types of Articles

- Refereed conference proceedings
- Refereed journal articles
- Review articles
- Letters

Types of Journals

Broadly two types of journals

1. "generalist" journals
2. "specialist" journals

For example, in science, *Nature* and *Science* are (high impact) generalist journals; *Journal of Plasma Physics* is a (lower impact) specialist journal.

1 Department of Agronomy, School of Agriculture, Lovely Professional University, Jalandhar, Punjab, India, 144411
2 Divison of Research and Development, Lovely Professional University, Jalandhar, Punjab, India, 144411

Impact Factor

Thomson Reuters (formerly ISI) *Journal Citation Reports web page:*

The journalimpact factor is a measure of the frequency with which the "average article" in a journal has been cited in a particular year.

The impact factor will help you to evaluate a journal's relative importance, especially when you compare it to others in the same field.

Impact Factor

$$\text{Impact Factor} = \frac{\text{no. of citations}}{\text{total no. of articles published}}$$

Calculated over the last 2 years.

Fig. 2.1: Impact factor calculation

(**Source:** based on review of literature)

Impact Factor

An example follows for the *Journal of Applied Physics*:

- In year 2015, the *Journal of Applied Physics* **received 152 citations to items published in (2014) and 183 citations to items published in (2013). Total citations for Impact Factor calculation = 335.**
- 123 source items were published in the *Journal of Applied Physics* **in (2014), and 108 in (2013).**
- Total source items for Impact Factor calculation = 231.

* Year 2015 Impact Factor for the *Journal of Applied Physics* **= 335/231 = 1.450.**

Impact Factor

Funding agencies and grant "assessors" may use the impact factor of journals in which you publish as an indicator of the quality of your work (i.e. they may form an opinion of the value of your work without actually reading it).

h-Index

- An index to quantify an individual's scientific research output
- Impact Factor is just for journals
- Combines an assessment of both quantity (number of papers) and quality (impact, or citations to these papers).
- *h*-index is automatically calculated:

  - *Web of Science, Scopus,* Publish or Perish (free download), based on data in *Google Scholar*
- *h-index* can also be manually calculated for an author

What is Research?

- Research is a process to discover new knowledge.
- The systematic investigation into and study of materials, sources, etc, in order to establish facts and reach new conclusions.
- An endeavour to discover new facts by the scientific study of a subject or by a course of critical investigation.

Starting Steps

- First step is to identify the research topic/field
- Formulate your question/problem
- Then figure out how you are going to answer it
  - How have others answered it?
  - How does your proposal fit in with what others have done?
  - How will you know when you have answered it?
- Then you can present your answer

Developing Your Question

- Start with a clear purpose
- Know your literature
- Be iterative in your approach
- Try to specify the who, what, where and when of your purpose
- Objective is intended to describe the purpose with a full statement of the research question

The Research Process

1. Identification of general problem/question
2. Literature review
3. Specify questions/hypotheses
4. Determination of design/methodology
5. Data collection
6. Data analysis/presentation
7. Interpretation of findings

Hypothesis

- Probability of research
  - Nothing is certain
  - Scientific "truth" is actually usually a statement of what is most probable given the currently known data within the given framework

- Statistical techniques try to help us show extent to which our results really do support the hypothesis

Targeting Journals

Factors you might consider when selecting a journal to submit to:

- Does your paper contain new knowledge or a new work or new idea?
- If your answer to this question is NO, then you must start again (most journals will quickly reject submissions of this type).
- Is your paper of very general interest / significance?
- Is it of more interest to a specialist group?

If the former, your work might be appropriate for a high-impact generalist journal; if the latter, it may be appropriate to target a good quality specialist journal.

What Publishers Want

They want well-written submissions that:

(*i*) Fall clearly within the field(s) prescribed by the journal (see the journal web site for this information).

(*ii*) Provide an advance knowledge.

Your manuscript will be more desirable to the editor if it contains a "big" advance in knowledge and/or addresses a current and topical area.

Scientific Research Article

- Provide a method for scientists to communicate with other scientists about their research.
- A standard format is used for the article, in which the author presents the research in an orderly and logical manner.
- This doesn't necessarily reflect the order in which you did or thought about the work.
- What will you do for.
- writing a quality research paper.

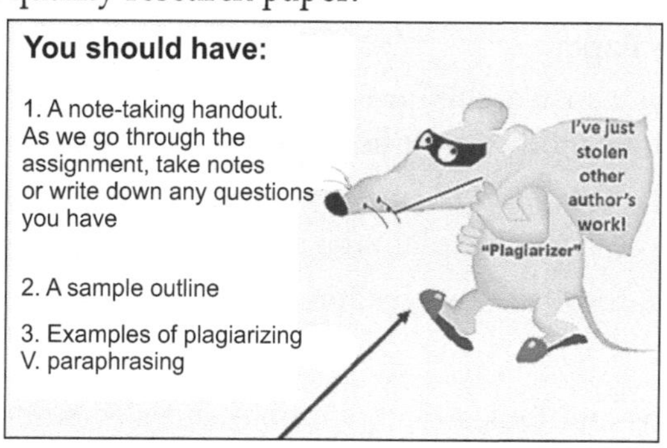

Fig. 2.2: Before research paper writing

(**Source:** based on review of literature)

While writing your research paper: Follow these instructions!

1. Your outline should be written before you start your paper. It organizes your thoughts and creates a plan so you know how your paper will look.
2. Your introduction tells the audience what you will explain in your paper. It will let the audience know what to expect from reading your paper.

Title

- Make your title specific enough to describe the contents of the paper, but not so technical that only specialists will understand.
- The title should be appropriate for the intended audience.
- The title usually describes the subject matter of the article.

Abstract

- The abstract should be a little less technical than the article itself.
- Your abstract should be one paragraph, of 100-250 words, which summarizes the purpose, methods, results and conclusions of the paper.
- It is not easy to include all this information in just a few words.
- Don't use abbreviations or citations in the abstract. It should be able to stand alone without any footnotes.

Introduction

- What question did you ask in your experiment/theory?
- Why is it interesting?
- The introduction summarizes the relevant literature so that the reader will understand why you were interested in the question you asked.
- One to four paragraphs should be enough. End with a sentence explaining the specific question you asked in this experiment/theory.

Main Body of the Paper

- How did you answer this question? There should be enough information here to allow another scientist to repeat your work.
- If you had a complicated protocol, it may helpful to include a diagram, table or flowchart to explain the methods you used.
- Do not put results in this section.

Results

- Use graphs and tables if appropriate, but also summarize your main findings in the text.
- Do NOT discuss the results here that goes in the Discussion.

- Use appropriate methods of showing data. Don't try to manipulate the data to make it look like you did more than you actually did.

Discussion

- Highlight the most significant results, but don't just repeat what you've written in the Results section.
- How do these results relate to the original question?
- Do the data support your hypothesis?
- Are your results consistent with what other investigators have reported?
- If your results were unexpected, try to explain why. Is there another way to interpret your results?
- What further research would be necessary to answer the questions raised by your results?
- How do your results fit into the big picture?
- End with a one-sentence summary of your conclusion, emphasizing why it is relevant.

References

- There are several possible ways to organize this section.
- It depends up on the journal in which you intend to submit your research.
- References should be written in the uniform manner as prescribed by the journal.
- This gives the authors of your sources credit for their work.
- P. X. Wang, Y. Nishida, N. Yugami, H. Ito, J. X. Wang, and S. Scheid, *J. Appl. Phys.* **91**, 856 (2002).
- G. Zeng, *Phys. Rev. E* **60**, 5950 (1999).
- G. Malka, E. Lefebvre, and J. L. Miquel, *Phys. Rev. Lett.* **78**, 3314 (1997).

Fig. 2.3: Plagiarism

(**Source:** based on review of literature)

Proofread !!!

1. Are all words spelled correctly?
2. Did I capitalize the beginning of each sentence and all proper nouns?
3. Did I punctuate correctly?
4. Do I use grammar correctly?
5. Did I answer all of the topic questions, and fulfill all of the requirements on my rubric.
6. Did I type the paper using the correct font type, size, line spacing and margin requirements?
7. Did I paraphrase all content?
8. Do my sentences make sense when read aloud?
9. Have I had my paper peer edited?
10. Does my paper flow well?
11. Did I include a bibliography page?

Criteria Used by Editors

Most good journals receive many more submissions that they can publish. Thus, the editors can usually afford to be *verychoosy*.

Key Features of Well Written Articles

A clear, concise and meaningful title which *creates interest.*

An Introduction that briefly provides a context for the work presented and *explicitly identifies the gap in knowledge addressed.*

If appropriate:

Detailed descriptions of materials and methods used (sufficient for other researchers to reproduce your work).

Results presented in a logical and clear way.

Key Features of Well Written Articles

A *critical and scholarly* Discussion of the state of the field and the contribution of this piece of work to the advancement of knowledge

e.g. What are the (*i*) implications of your results? and (*ii*) limitations of previous work and of the current report?

What needs to be done in the future to solve remaining uncertainties?

The Writing Process

Practical Tips:

Actively seek out *critical* readers (co-authors or peers) to provide comments on your drafts.

Have a Mentor

Try and anticipate points of criticism from reviewers

First article, 5-10 drafts

Best Articles, 2-4 rejections

Conclusion

- Journal impact factor is used to categorize good journals
- Don't use Journal Impact Factors to evaluate individuals. Perhaps use *h-index*, instead?
- When considering where to publish, besides Journal Impact Factor of the journal also consider:
  - International reach
  - Where or if it's indexed
  - Openly accessible?
  - Readership numbers
  - Subject appropriateness
- Each part of the manuscript is important and should be taken carefully.
- Abstract should be precise and informative.
- Highlight the innovative part of your investigation and its relevance.
- Plagiarism need to be checked before submission.

REFERENCES

https://www.aresearchguide.com/1steps.html

https://writing.wisc.edu/Handbook/PlanResearchPaper.html

https://writing.wisc.edu/handbook/assignments/planresearchpaper/

https://owl.purdue.edu/owl/general_writing/...writing.../research_papers/index.html

Scientific Writing and Research Quality **Pages 18-25**
Edited by: Dr. Prasann Kumar & Dr. Pawan Kumar 'Bharti'
ISBN: 978-93-88854-48-1
Edition: 2020
Published by: Discovery Publishing House Pvt. Ltd., New Delhi (India)

3

Research Design
Fundamental Key for Innovative Research

Prasann Kumar[1,2]* & Shipa Rani Dey[1]

GRAPHICAL ABSTRACT

Keywords: *Design, Fundamental, Innovative, Key, Research*

Introduction

Knowledge is continually evolving. What was believed to be true yesterday may be doubted today, scorned tomorrow, and resurrected in the future. Just as knowledge itself evolves, beliefs about how to create knowledge also evolve. Our beliefs about the methods of obtaining knowledge constitute research paradigms.

- There are various classification systems and it is even possible to combine aspects of different study types to create new research designs.
- For this FDP we will classify into following types (Creswell, 2009).
  - Quantitative Methods.
  - Qualitative Methods.

[1] Department of Agronomy, School of Agriculture, Lovely Professional University, Jalandhar, Punjab, India, 144411
[2] Divison of Research and Development, Lovely Professional University, Jalandhar, Punjab, India, 144411

– Mixed Methods.

- These methods are sometimes referred to as research paradigms.

ASSUSMPTIONS OF THE THREE RESEARCH PARADIGMS

Assumption	PARADIGM		
	Quantitative	Qualitative	Single-Subject
Reality	Single, objective	Multiple, constructed	Single, Objective
Relationship between investigator and subject	Independent	Dependent	Independent
Generalizability of findings	Desirable and possible	Situation specific	System Specific
Cause-and-effect relationships	Causal	Noncausal	Causal
Values	Value free	Value bound	Value free

Fig. 3.1: Paradigm-Assumption, Quantitative and Qualitative

(**Source:** based on review of literature)

Definition

- Research Designs are plans and the procedures for research that span the decision from broad assumptions to detailed methods of data collection and analysis (Creswell, 2009).
- A design is a way of arranging the environment **in** which a survey takes place. The environment consists of the individuals or groups of people, places activities, or objects that are to be surveyed (Fink, 2002).
- Three components involved in a design
- Philosophical assumptions
- Strategies of inquiry
- Specific methods

Strategies of Inquiry

Strategies of inquiry are types of qualitative, quantitative, and mixed methods designs or models that provide specific direction for procedures in a research design.

ALTERNATIVE STRATEGIES OF INQUIRY

Quantitative	Qualitative	Mixed Methods
• Experimental designs • Non-experlrnental designs, such as surveys	• Narrative research • Phenomenology • Ethnographies • Grounded theory studies • Case study	• Sequential • Concurrent • Transformative

Fig. 3.2: Alternative strategy of Inquiry

(**Source:** based on review of literature)

Research Methods

- The third major element in the framework is the specific research methods that involve the forms of data collection, analysis, and interpretation that researchers propose for their studies.

METHODS OF THE THREE RESEARCH PARADIGMS

Method	PARADIGM		
	Quantitative	Qualitative	Single-Subject
Theory	A priori	Grounded	A priori
Number of selection of subjects	Groupds, random	Small number, purposive	One, purposive
Measurement tools	Instruments	Human	Instruments
Type of data	Numerical	Language	Numerical
Manipulation	Present	Absent	Present
Control	Maximized	Minimized	Flexible

Fig. 3.3: Paradigm-method, quantitative and qualitative

(**Source:** based on review of literature)

Criteria for Selecting a Research Approach

- Research Problem
- The personal experiences of the researcher

The audience(s) for whom the report will be written

Population and Samples

- A **population** is the total group of interest.
- A **sample** is a subgroup of that interest.
- **Sampling** is the procedure by which a sample of units or elements is selected from a population.
- In clinical research, sampling unit may be the individual or a group of related individuals.

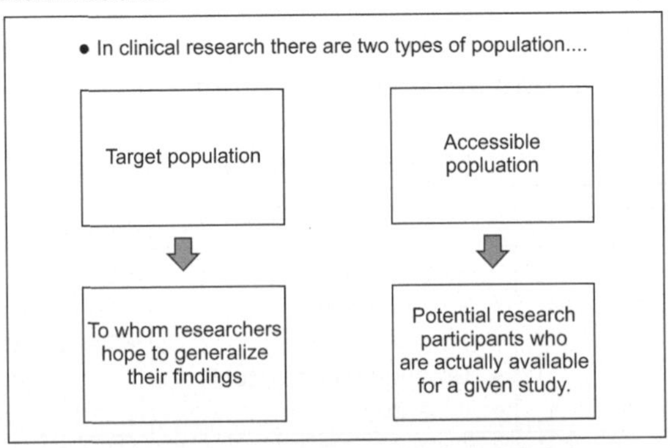

Fig. 3.4: Clinical research and population

(**Source:** based on review of literature)

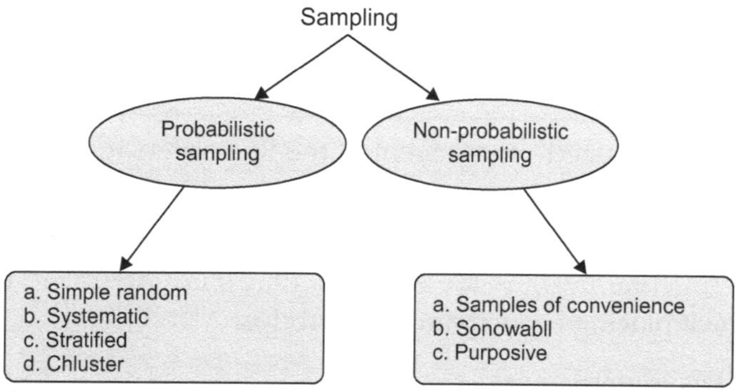

Fig. 3.5: Sampling

(**Source:** based on review of literature)

Experimental Research Designs

- Characterized by controlled manipulation of an active independent variable or variables by researchers
- Based on the treatment of data they are classified as
    - Group Designs
    - Single subject Designs

RESEARCH DESIGN

Method	Experimental		Non-experimental		
Type	**True**	**Qual**	**Descriptive**	**Exploratory**	**Analytical**
Design	Pro-post test control group	One group pre-post test	Survey	Cohort	Systematic Review
	Post- tost only control group	One-way repeated measures	Nomative	Case Control	Meta-Analysia
	Multi-factorial	Two-group pre-post test	Observational	Epider-original	
	Mixed Design	Two-way repealed measures	Developmental	Correlation	
		Non-equiva-lent pre-post test control	Case	Meltodol-ogical	
		Historical control	Qualitative		
		Cross-over design			
		Single subject designs			

Fig. 3.6: Research Designs

(**Source:** based on review of literature)

Randomized Controlled Trial

- They are basically used to determining whether clinical interventions work.
- The "randomized" component of the RCT refers to random allocation of participants to treatment and control groups.
- Remember all RCTs are experimental designs, however, not all experimental designs are RCTs, in that there are many non-random ways of placing participants into groups.

Efficacy Versus Effectiveness

- Archie Cochrane, British famous clinical epidemiologist, defined two concepts related to assessing healthcare interventions.
- Efficacy is the extent to which an intervention does more good than harm under ideal circumstances.
- Effectiveness assesses whether an intervention does more good than harm when provided under usual circumstances of healthcare practice.

Group Designs

- Single Factor
- Multiple Factor

SINGLE FACTOR EXPERIMENTAL DESIGNS

- Pretest-Posttest Control-Group Design
- Other name is parallel Group Design

R O × O
R O   O

Fig. 3.7: Single factor experimental designs

(**Source:** based on review of literature)

SINGLE FACTOR EXPERIMENTAL DESIGNS

- Posttest-Only Control-Group Design

R O × O
R O   O

Fig. 3.8: Continuation of figure 3.7

(**Source:** based on review of literature)

SINGLE FACTOR EXPERIMENTAL DESIGNS

- Single-Group pretest-Posttest Design

O × O

Fig. 3.9: Continuation of figure 3.8

(**Source:** based on review of literature)

SINGLE FACTOR EXPERIMENTAL DESIGNS

- Nonequivalent Control-Group Design
- The nonequivalent control-group design is used when a nonrandom control group is available for comparison.

O × O
- - - - - -
O   O

Fig. 3.10: Continuation of figure 3.9

(**Source:** based on review of literature)

- Time Series Design
- The time series design is used to establish a baseline of measurements before initiation of treatment to either a group or an individual.
- The number of measurements taken before, after, or even during the intervention varies depending on the nature of the study, O O O O X O O O O.

A great difficulty in developing...clinical science...is that we treat individual persons, each of whom is made up of situations which are unique and, there-lore, appear incompatible with the generalizations demanded of science. 1(i)[1076)]

Fig. 3.11: Single Subject Design

(**Source:** based on review of literature)

When to use Single-Subject Design

- A single-subject design may be used where withholding treatment is considered unethical, or random assignment of subjects may not be possible.

Single Subject: Why?

- Identify effective interventions in natural settings for individuals
- Effective defined by clinical significance rather then clinical significance

- Only need 1 participant
- Can have maximum up to 8 (Horner, 2005)

Single Subject Design

- Single-subject designs are often confused with clinical case reports or case studies.
- The two are very different.

Characteristics of Single Subject Design

- Baseline Assessment
- Stability of performance
- Continuous Assessment
- Use of different phases

Single Subject Design

- The following are the five basic forms of single subject design
- A-B Designs
- Withdrawal Designs
- Multiple-Baseline Designs
- Alternating-Treatment Designs

Changing-Criterion Designs

Observational Studies

- Descriptive
- Exploratory
- Analytical

Descriptive Observational Studies

- Survey
- Normative
- Developmental
- Case Designs (case reports, case studies, and case series)

Exploratory Observational Studies

- Cohort
- Case Control
- Ecological Studies
- Correlation Studies
- Methodological

Analytical Studies

- Systematic Reviews
- Meta Analysis

Conclusion

A **research design** is the set of methods and procedures used in collecting and analyzing measures of the variables specified in the problem research. The design of a study defines the study type (descriptive, correlation, semi-experimental, experimental, review, meta-analytic) and sub-type (e.g., descriptive-longitudinal case study), research problem, hypotheses, independent and dependent variables, experimental design, and, if applicable, data collection methods and a statistical analysis plan. A research design is a framework that has been created to find answers to research questions.

REFERENCES

https://en.wikipedia.org/wiki/Research_design

https://www.questionpro.com › Home › Consumer Insights › Market Research

https://libguides.usc.edu/writingguide/researchdesigns

https://explorable.com/research-designs

https://guides.lib.vt.edu/researchmethods/design-method

https://www.nyu.edu/classes/bkg/methods/005847ch1.pdf

https://cirt.gcu.edu/research/developmentresources/research.../quantresearch/approach.

https://www.scribbr.com › Knowledge Base › Starting the research process

https://scholarshipfellow.com › Blog

https://library.sacredheart.edu/c.php?g=29803&p=185902

Scientific Writing and Research Quality **Pages 26-33**
Edited by: Dr. Prasann Kumar & Dr. Pawan Kumar 'Bharti'
ISBN: 978-93-88854-48-1
Edition: 2020
Published by: Discovery Publishing House Pvt. Ltd., New Delhi (India)

4

Topic for Research
Key for Sustainable Work in Agriculture

Prasann Kumar[1,2]* & Shipa Rani Dey[1]

GRAPHICAL ABSTRACT

Keywords: *Agriculture, Crop, Forage, Gap, Sustainable, Research*

Introduction

Why selection of topic is so important

- It create interest among the researcher
- to make a significant contribution to the field of study
- to publish your work
- to the competition for good grades and higher education

Choosing a subject or area of interest

- Initial step in the research process is to decide on a tentative subject or area of interest.

[1] Department of Agronomy, School of Agriculture, Lovely Professional University, Jalandhar, Punjab, India, 144411
[2] Divison of Research and Development,, Lovely Professional University, Jalandhar, Punjab, India, 144411

- To have a very general idea of what you'd like to pursue.
- For example, you may decide you'd like to research migration, alcoholism, freedom of speech, archaeology, social support, climate change, or feminist literature.
- Merely choosing a broad subject area from which you can able to shape a precise research topic.
- If you are unable to come up with a broad subject area, here are some suggestions that may spark ideas.
- Choose a subject that interests you. The more curiosity you have about an area, the more enthusiasm and motivation.
- Browsing your textbook, lecture notes, current magazines and newspapers, and annual review sources (yearbooks, e.g.) may give your ideas.
- Ask experts

Turning an Interest into a Topic

- "Nothing contributes to the quality of your work more than your commitment to it".
- The best way to start is to read books on the topic.
- You can also talk to others about the topic (e.g., fellow students, others interested in that area, or experts).
- You should then look at the primary literature (i.e., journals) to see who is writing about this topic. Why are they so interested in the topic?
- With the initial scoping complete, you can turn to the Internet to find out more about your topic.

Process/Steps in Topic Selection

- Brainstorm for ideas
- Read general background information
- Focus in on a manageable topic
- Make a list of useful keywords
- Be flexible
- Conduct a Literature Search: Does the existing literature address the topic?
- Identify a Research Question: What are your variables going to be?

Brainstorm for ideas

- Use the following questions to help you generate topic ideas.
  - Do you have a strong opinion on a current social or political controversy?

  - Did you read a newspaper article, or see a TV broadcast recently that piqued your curiosity or made you angry or anxious?
  - Is there an aspect of one of your courses you are interested in learning more about?

Read general background information

- Reading a broad summary enables you to get an overview of the topic and see how your idea relates to broader, narrower and related issues.
- Use article databases to scan current magazine, journal or newspaper articles on the topic.
- Browse govt. websites/search engine relevant to your field.

Focus in on a manageable topic

- Keep it manageable. A topic will be very difficult to research if it is too broad, or too narrow. One way to narrow a broad topic such as "the environment" is to limit your topic. Common ways to limit a topic are:
  - by geographic region

    Example: What environmental issues are most important in the Punjab?
  - by culture

    Example: How does the environment fit into the youth life view?
  - by time frame

    Example: What are the most prominent environmental issues of the last 10 years?
  - by discipline

    Example: How does environmental awareness effect business practices today?
  - by population group

    Example: What are the effects of air pollution on senior's citizens?
- Remember that a topic will be more difficult to research if it is too:
  - Locally confined - Topics this specific may only be covered in local newspapers, if at all!

    Example: What sources of pollution affect the chaheru village?
  - Recent - Be aware if a topic is very recent. (books and journal articles will not be available)

    Example: Events that happened yesterday or last week
  - Broadly interdisciplinary - You could be overwhelmed with superficial information

    Example: How can the environment contribute to the culture, politics and society of the Northern states?

Make a list of useful keywords

- Keep track of the words that are used to describe your topic.
  - Look for words that best describe your topic.
  - These words will be found in the encyclopaedia articles and other reading you do while selecting your topic.
  - Find synonyms, broader and narrower terms for each keyword you find in order to expand your search capabilities.

Be flexible

- It is common to modify your topic during the research process.
  - You can never be sure of what you may find.
  - You may find too much and need to narrow your focus, or too little and need to broaden your focus. This is a normal part of the research process.
  - When researching, you may not wish to change your topic, but you may decide that some other aspect of the topic is more interesting or manageable.

Conduct a literature search: Does the existing literature address the topic?

- It is much easier to design a good study and choose appropriate methods to do so when you can refer to the research done by other scholars.
- Pay close attention to discussion sections where authors often include a critique of their own work in which they identify limitations of the design and its implications for further study.

Identify a Research Question

- Once, review of literature is done, you will have a pretty clear picture of what you want to study, and possibly even how you are going to study.
- Your research question is exactly what it sounds like – a statement about the relationship between two variables.
- For ex. To what extent does age at marriage influence divorce?

Useful website/journals to refer for selection of topic

- Govt. websites:
  - ICSSR, UGC, ICMR, Department of social welfare, National commission of Women, Ministry of Family welfare, etc.,
- Research institutes
  - ISEC, TISS, NIRD, IIPS,IIPA,ICHR,IIPR, **Indian Institute** of Remote Sensing (IIRS), CLAI

- Journals in your respective field
  - EPW, Sage, Routlege, Taylor and Francis, Emerald, Spengler,

Summary

- Think of the who, what, when, where and why questions:
  - WHY did you choose the topic? What interests you about it? Do you have an opinion about the issues involved?
  - WHO are the information providers on this topic? Who might publish information about it? Who is affected by the topic? Do you know of organizations or institutions affiliated with the topic?
  - WHAT are the major questions for this topic? Is there a debate about the topic? Are there a range of issues and viewpoints to consider?
  - WHERE is your topic important: at the local, national or international level? Are there specific places affected by the topic?
  - WHEN is/was your topic important? Is it a current event or an historical issue? Do you want to compare your topic by time periods?

Exercise

- Area of Interest: Gerontological studies
- Tentative Topic: A study on Socio-economic condition of Rural Elderly Women
- Sources: Center for Gerontological studies, Sage publication, Taylor and Francis
- Focus: Rural, Women

Key Words: Elderly Women, Income, Housing, Recreation

Review

- Depression among the Rural Elderly A Study of Prevalence and Correlates.
- Access to health care for the rural elderly.
- Retirement satisfaction in the rural elderly.
- Mini Nutritional Assessment of rural elderly people in Bangladesh: the impact of demographic, socio-economic and health factors.
- Family support, financial needs, and health care needs of rural elderly in China: A field study
  - Research Question: Which age group of elderly women faces more socio-economic problem?
  - Final Topic: Socio-economic condition of Rural Elderly women in Mana Block of Fategarh District

How to Write a Project Proposal

Proposal/synopsis

It is a systematic plan, which brings to focus the preliminary planning that will be needed to accomplish the purpose of the proposed study.

Purpose of preparation:

- For completing/getting diplomas/degrees.
- For getting financial assistance for quality research (external and internal sources).

Proposal writing

- What is the point?
- Use a clear writing style
- Get the correct format
- Put all the bits in place
- Leave enough time to polish the document

Why work to perfect the art of proposal writing?

- Organize your thinking
- Communicate your expertise
- Impress and conquer
- Get the job done!

Four things never to do:

- Do not plagiarise. This means a good bye to the cut copy and paste culture.
- Do not take credit for other person's work and therefore citations are compulsory.
- Never have an average of less than 3 references per A/4 page unless you want to submit a substandard work.
- Do not set out to change the world by making pronouncements from the pulpit. Always rely on empirical data that can be tested, validated and make sure that correlation does not amount to causation.

Four things to consider doing:

- Narrow down the scope of your inquiry and go deep into its background. The wider your ambit the vaguer your analysis may be.
- Be very careful and avoid the fallacy of composition and fallacy of accident(controversial issues).
- Start collecting your citations (in full) on cards or a notebook from day one as you may have to travel the same path to give the bibliographical references when you are done.

- Select a scientific methodology and stick to it. There is absolutely no substitute for empirical and/or logical rigour.

What is a project proposal?

A project proposal presents a project by outlining:

- The specific objectives of the project.
- The technical approach to be used in solving the problem
- The anticipated results of the project

Project proposals should answer the following questions:

- Is the problem sufficiently important to justify money, time and effort?
- Is the project well defined and realistic?
- Have you outlined a sound approach, including your ability to perform the tasks?

Why write a project proposal?

- To inform people or organizations of a project that you would like to implement.
- To apply for a grant.
- To ask for other resources or support from another organization.
- To explore the causes of a problem and clearly define next steps in solving that problem.

Funding Agencies/Sources

All possible funding sources

- GovernmentSources
- National Foundations
- Regional Foundations
- Corporations
- Donors

Funding agencies

- UGC
- ICSSR
- NCTE
- NCERT
- Ministries (Govt. of India)

Type of research project

- Minor research project (time duration, funds and discipline)
- Major research project (time duration, funds and discipline)

Before writing a project proposal...

- Write a concept paper.
- Identify funding agency.
- Identify the priority area of funding agency matching your focused area.
- Make a multidisciplinary/multi-institutional team.
- Discuss the concept paper with concerned person in funding agency to achieve funding agency targets and level of funding.
- Formulation of project in the format of funding agency.

Components of project proposal

- Cover Page
- Introduction
  - Background/Need
  - Statement of the Problem
  - Rationale/Justification and Intervention
- Objectives
- Methodology(Intervention Design and Strategy
- Activities and Timeline
- Budget
- Evaluation Indicators
- Bibliography
- Annex

Cover page

- Title: Title gives first impression of a proposal and hence it has to be catchy, small and informative. It shall not be same as objective, it has to be shorter but at the same time indicates broadly what is being attempted and corresponding to the theme of the intervention.
- Institution Information.
- Author.
- Date.

REFERENCES

https://www.aresearchguide.com/1steps.html

https://writing.wisc.edu/Handbook/PlanResearchPaper.html

https://writing.wisc.edu/handbook/assignments/planresearchpaper/

https://owl.purdue.edu/owl/general_writing/...writing.../research_papers/index.html

Scientific Writing and Research Quality **Pages 34-47**
Edited by: Dr. Prasann Kumar & Dr. Pawan Kumar 'Bharti'
ISBN: 978-93-88854-48-1
Edition: 2020
Published by: Discovery Publishing House Pvt. Ltd., New Delhi (India)

5

How to Write an Effective Report in Science?

Prasann Kumar[1,2]* & Shipa Rani Dey[1]

GRAPHICAL ABSTRACT

Keywords: *Conferences, Documents, Paper, Research, Science*

Introduction

- It is obvious that every research needs good and proper documentation.
- To attend conferences.
- To share research results with other researchers.
- To get views for improvement of your research.
- To obtain some form of degree.
- To get recognition and promotion

High Quality Research

- It is based on the work of others.
- It can be replicated (duplicated).
- It is generalizable to other settings.

1 Department of Agronomy, School of Agriculture, Lovely Professional University, Jalandhar, Punjab, India, 144411
2 Divison of Research and Development, Lovely Professional University, Jalandhar, Punjab, India, 144411

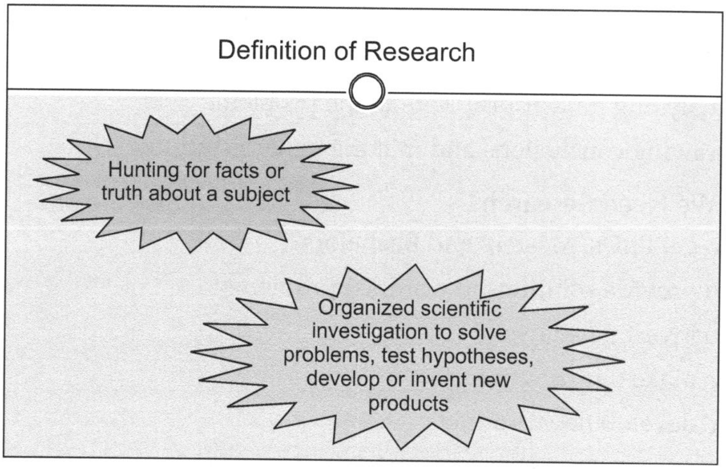

Fig. 5.1: Definition of Research

(**Source:** based on review of literature)

- It is based on some logical rationale and tied to theory.
- It is doable!
- It generates new questions or is cyclical in nature.
- It is incremental.
- It is a political activity that should be undertaken for the betterment of society

Then, What is Bad Research?

- The opposites of what have been discussed.
- Looking for something when it simply is not to be found.
- Plagiarizing other people's work.
- Falsifying data to prove a point.
- Misrepresenting information and misleading participants.

What is Research?

Research must be systematic - It follows certain steps that are logical in order. These steps are:

- Understanding the nature of problem to be studied and identifying the related area of knowledge.
- Reviewing literature to understand how others have approached or dealt with the problem.

- Collecting data in an organized and controlled manner so as to arrive at valid decisions.
- Analyzing data appropriate to the problem.
- Drawing conclusions and making generalizations.

Why Do We Need Research?

- To get PhDs, Masters and Bachelors??
- To provide solutions to complex problems
- To investigate laws of nature
- To make new discoveries
- To develop new products
- To save costs
- To improve our life
- Human desires

Characteristics of Research

- Involve in the development of new algorithms/techniques/ methodologies.
- Involve in the confirmation of newly proposed algorithms (applications to benchmark problems or laboratory equipment).
- Involve in the design of new products/circuits.
- Involve in comparing a number of different methodologies.
- Stability analysis on newly proposed algorithms.
- Involve in the application of some proposed algorithms in novel applications.
- Involve in the study of certain aspects of dynamics (behavior) of plants/ systems.
- Involve in surveys of some engineering aspects.
- Involve in market study of certain engineering products.
- Involve in the study on the effects of environmental factors on a particular product/design.
- Involve in improving the design of existing products.
- Involve in extending the algorithms developed by others to a wider variety of applications/systems.
- Involve in the testing of new techniques extensively on benchmark problems in which earlier research has not done.

Major Differences Between Research Activities in the Engineering Discipline and Others

- Engineering research are more formulative in nature.
- A lot is based on mathematics.
- Experiments are conducted on machines, rather than humans or animals.
- Data to be collected differ significantly.
- Hypotheses arrived at are largely based on mathematicalproofs, rather than just an educated guess.
- Experiments can be done within a shorterperiod of time.
- Outputs in engineering research are moretangible such as a software, a new machine or component, or even mathematical equations, etc.

Library and Primary Research

- Library research refers to gathering information that others have generated.
- Primary research refers to generating information through data collection, analysis, and reporting findings.

Articles, Papers, or Research Reports Convey

- Facts and/or theories others in the research community generated (research reviews).
- Facts and/or theories the research community generated and one's own findings generated from a research project (research article or book).
- And rarely, only one's findings generated from a research project (applied research).
- Generally covers only one important topic of interest and conveys evidence and interpretations of evidence.
- Research reports are NOT creative writing, opinion pieces, poems, novels, letters, musings, memoirs, or interesting to read.

Quantitative Vs. Qualitative

- Qualitative Research
  - Designed to capture social life as participants experience it
  - Emphasis on subjective, meanings
- Quantitative Research
  - Designed to measure social variables, numerically
  - Emphasis on numerical summaries and interrelationship of phenomena

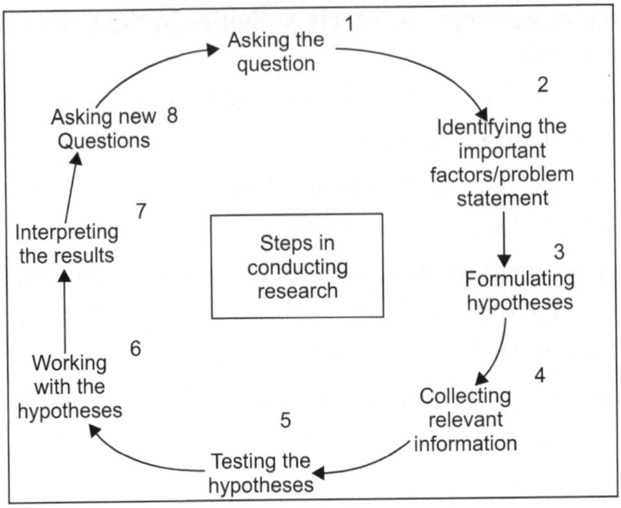

Fig. 5.2: Qualitative vs. quantitative research

(**Source:** based on review of literature)

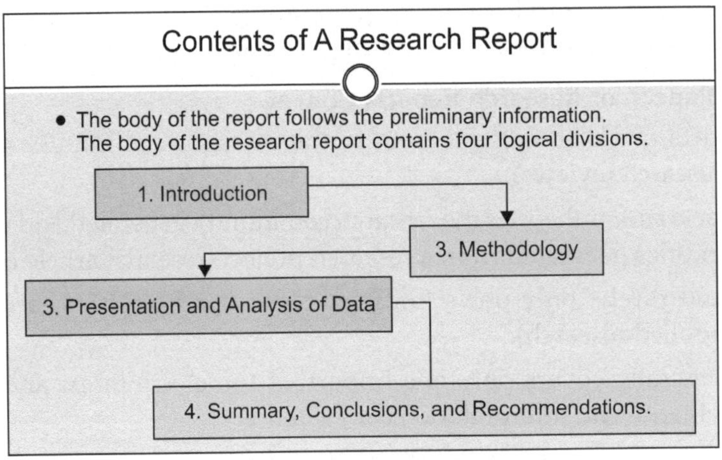

Fig. 5.3: Contents of a research reports

(**Source:** based on review of literature)

Components of Research

A research report has seven components:

1. Abstract or Summary
2. Introduction
3. Review of Literature
4. Methods
5. Results

6. Conclusions and Discussion
7. References

Abstract or Summary

- The abstract or summary tells the reader very briefly what the main points and findings of the paper are. It is a brief account of the paper's relevant points.
- Length and format are usually specified for a particular journal.
- It must stand alone without reference to text body.
- Should include some information on the results obtained.
- This allows the reader to decide whether the paper is useful to them.
- Get into the habit of reading only abstracts while searching for papers that are relevant to your research.
- Read the body of a paper only when you think it will be useful to you.

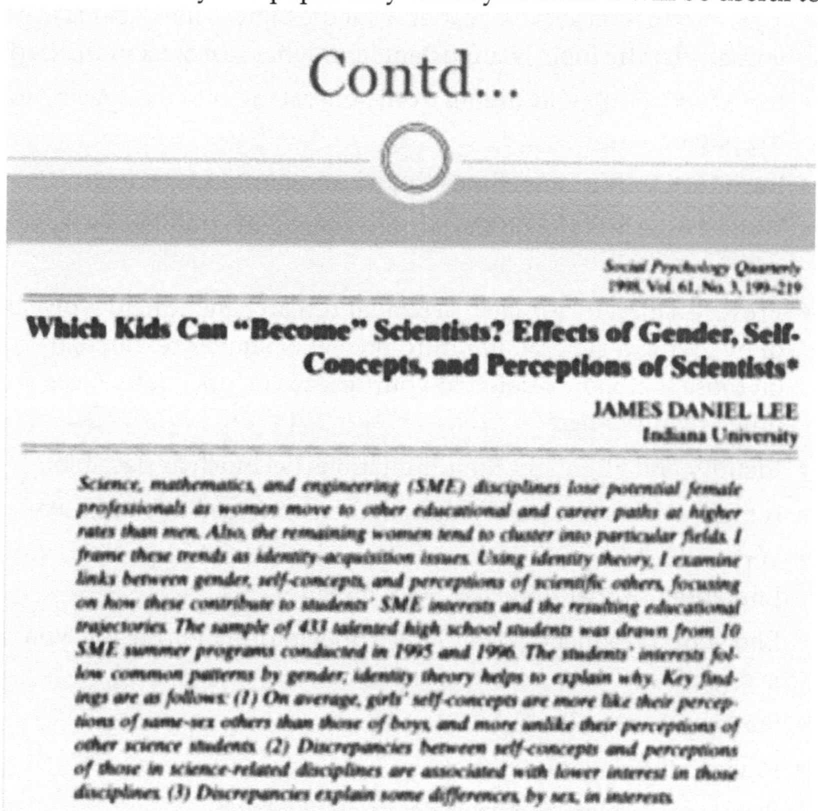
Contd...

Social Psychology Quarterly
1998, Vol. 61, No. 3, 199–219

Which Kids Can "Become" Scientists? Effects of Gender, Self-Concepts, and Perceptions of Scientists*

JAMES DANIEL LEE
Indiana University

Science, mathematics, and engineering (SME) disciplines lose potential female professionals as women move to other educational and career paths at higher rates than men. Also, the remaining women tend to cluster into particular fields. I frame these trends as identity-acquisition issues. Using identity theory, I examine links between gender, self-concepts, and perceptions of scientific others, focusing on how these contribute to students' SME interests and the resulting educational trajectories. The sample of 433 talented high school students was drawn from 10 SME summer programs conducted in 1995 and 1996. The students' interests follow common patterns by gender; identity theory helps to explain why. Key findings are as follows: (1) On average, girls' self-concepts are more like their perceptions of same-sex others than those of boys, and more unlike their perceptions of other science students. (2) Discrepancies between self-concepts and perceptions of those in science-related disciplines are associated with lower interest in those disciplines. (3) Discrepancies explain some differences, by sex, in interests

Fig. 5.4: Abstract or Summary

(**Source:** based on review of literature)

Abstract

The Fractal dimension technique is widely used nowadays in various wakes of engineering analysis. The aim of the paper is to demonstrate that the technique of fractal dimensions can be applied to fingerprint analysis. In this paper we propose an algorithm to quantify the fingerprint to a single number on the basis of Fractal theory. The algorithm was implemented using MATLAB and the results are reproduced. The algorithm will greatly reduce processing time as compared to conventional techniques. The paper presents a preliminary idea illustrating this concept and an example as to how it can be applied practically. We propose that the algorithm can be used to screen the number of possible matches for a fingerprint followed by pattern matching techniques to obtain the best match.

Introduction

- The introduction tells the reader what the topic of the paper is in general terms, why the topic is important, and what to expect in the paper.
- Introductions should funnel from general ideas to the specific topic of the paper.
- Introductions are sometimes folded into literature reviews.
- Write a brief account on the current state of the problems – Answer the why?
- Provide a literature review of similar research in the field- you can start of by giving a general literature review of similar research, then focus on those that more related to your research work – references are very much required here.
- Identify and Highlight their limitations (as much as possible).
- If there is not so much limitation –then you need to be creative.
- Write a brief account of your proposed technique and how the limitations as identified can be overcome.
- End your Introduction by writing a brief information on how your paper is organized.
- Statement of the Problem.
- Review of Related Literature.
- Statement of Hypotheses of Research Questions.
- Limitations.
- Definition of Terms.

Introduction–Example

This research focuses on sex differences in identity change processes. The identity theory perspective in sociology asserts that interaction may prompt change in inherently stable self-concepts. While research supports the general specifications of identity theory, the perspective makes no statement about whether identity processes are the same for each sex; researchers typically assume similarity. This issue remains to be systematically explored. Indeed, recent research on gender differences among science and technology students (Lee, 2002) calls for scrutiny of the assumption that females' and males* identities and behaviors respond to social relationships in the same way. The present research addresses this gap in the identity theory literature.

Fig. 5.5: Introduction –Example

(**Source:** based on review of literature)

Review Of Literature

- The literature review tells the reader what other researchers have discovered about the paper's topic or tells the reader about other research that is relevant to the topic.
- A literature review should shape the way readers think about a topic—it educates readers about what the community of scholars says about a topic and its surrounding issues.
- Often what students call a "research paper" is merely a review of literature.
- Along the way it states facts and ideas about the world and supports those facts and ideas with credit for where they came from.
- Irrelevant information is not discussed.
- The literature review has its own voice. The sources of information are not extensively quoted or "copied and pasted." Instead, the author puts facts and ideas into his or her own words while pointing out where the information came from. Literature reviews have parenthetical citations running throughout. These are part of a systematic way to document where facts and ideas came from, allowing the skeptical reader to look up anything that is questionable.
- Parenthetical citation is our way of substantiating claims we made in our own words, without breaking our flow.
- Each citation directs the reader to the references where complete details on sources can be found.
- Citations consist of authors' last names and the year of publication. One finds complete information on sources by looking up last names

and dates in alphabetized references—so there's no need to put all that information in the text.

- We have conventions that allow the reader to figure out where information is coming from.
- In text, just pointing out where info came from:
- blahblah (Author Year) or (Lee 2004).
- In text, where you quoted someone:
- "Quote quote" (Author Year: Pages) or (Lee 2004: 340).
- In text, more than one source:
- (Author Year; Author Year) or (Lee 2004; Seymour & Hewitt 1997)
- In text, if you want to use the author's name in a sentence:
- Author (Year) says that... or Lee (2004) claims that girls...
- Quoting a person and using their name:
- Author (Year: Pages) says, "Quote quote..." or Lee (2004: 341) says, "Girls are more likely to..."

Literature Review – Examples

Various identities. Consequently, she may change her career plans like the college women discussed by Rayman and brett (1993-61) who "appeared to to have discovered new sides to themselves. They participated in extracurricular activities, studied somewhat less than others and found they were attractive to others, "Similarly, serpe and stryker (1987) found that, upon entering college, women are more likely than men to construct new selves. One may expect a similar

Actors behave in ways that confirm self meanings (Banaji and Prentice 1994: Stryker 1968, 1980; Swan. Stein-Serousssi, and Giesler 1992). In fact, fact, Burke (1991 b) asserts that stress is created by a meanings discrepancy between one's internal standard and the feedback one receives from social activity.

Fig. 5.6: Literature Review Example

(**Source:** based on review of literature)

Proposed Technique and Method

- Can be divided into several sub-sections
- Provide a general description of the technique or method you proposed (use block diagrams where appropriate)
- In another section, start with the general theory first then followed by your own formulations

- Write down your algorithms (equations)/strategy and provide explanation on them
- Figures may be required where necessary

Hardware/Software Development

- As a result of your proposed algorithm, you might have developed a software to test its viability through simulation
- Provide a description of how the software is developed (Computer specs, Programming Languages used, Flowcharts, Block diagrams, etc.)
- Sometimes hardware are designed to test the proposed technique/ algorithm
- Provide sufficient description of the hardware setup/ designed (technical specifications, block diagrams, saturations, sensor limitations, components used, photos of the hardware, etc.)
- Highlight the uniqueness of your hardware compared to similar products (if any)

Application of the Technique/Algorithm

- Usually new techniques/algorithms are tested using programs – simulations
- Test-beds are usually bench-marked problems in the form of equations
- Provide a write-up on how the simulation is carried up (including all assumptions used, how important parameters are chosen/selected, etc.)
- Similarly for hardware application, describe how the experiments have been carried out
- Only discuss experiments which are relevant to show the effectiveness or superiority of the proposed technique

A Methods Section Must Contain

- Descriptions of Data
  - Think in terms of: "Who, What, When, Where, Why and How?"
  - Target Population
  - The Ways Data were Collected:
    * Sampling
    * Delivery Methods
  - Response Rates

- Limitations of Data (Who is omitted, biases)
- Any analyses necessary to bolster claims the data are appropriate
- Sample sizes through various decisions
  * Such as:
    - eliminating non-Christians from the sample
    - using only white respondents

Results

The results section chronicles the findings of the statistical analyses and assesses whether your expectations (hypotheses) were correct.

The results section includes:

- Professional tables showing descriptive and inferential statistics
- Narrative describing most relevant findings
- The narrative and tables are complementary.
  - The narrative discusses ONLY VERY IMPORTANT findings and refers to where information can be found in the tables as different facts are discussed.
  - The tables contain almost all statistical information so that the author does not have to write a narrative for every detail in the analysis.

The results section includes:

- Evaluations of the hypotheses. Were the research hypotheses supported?
- Statements about new discoveries or surprises encountered in the analyses
- Results can be tabulated in several forms (use graphical form where applicable)
- Usually comparisons with existing techniques (conventional or otherwise) are required to show the effectiveness of the proposed technique
- Provide merit discussions – correct analyses of your experimental results show the quality of the paper. Always provide answers to why the experiments went such a way.
- Every figure shown in the paper must be addressed in the text. Figures must be legible enough.
- What conclusion can you draw from your experiments?

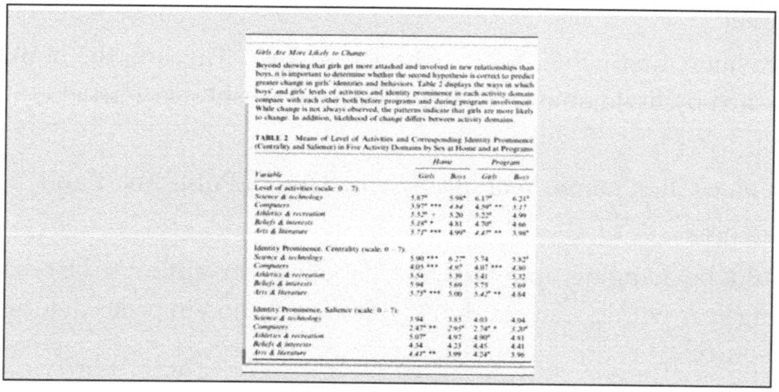

Girls Are More Likely to Change

Beyond showing that girls get more attached and involved in new relationships than boys, it is important to determine whether the second hypothesis is correct to predict greater change in girls' identities and behaviors. Table 2 displays the ways in which boys' and girls' levels of activities and identity prominence in each activity domain compare with each other both before programs and during program involvement. While change is not always observed, the patterns indicate that girls are more likely to change. In addition, likelihood of change differs between activity domains.

TABLE 2 Means of Level of Activities and Corresponding Identity Prominence (Centrality and Salience) in Five Activity Domains by Sex at Home and at Programs

Variable	Home		Program	
	Girls	Boys	Girls	Boys
Level of activities (scale: 0 – 7):				
Science & technology	5.87ª	5.98ª	6.17ª	6.21ª
Computers	3.97ª ***	4.84	4.59ª **	5.17
Athletics & recreation	5.52ª +	5.20	5.22ª	4.99
Beliefs & interests	5.18ª *	4.81	4.70ª	4.66
Arts & literature	5.71ª ***	4.99ª	4.47ª **	3.98ª
Identity Prominence, Centrality (scale: 0 – 7):				
Science & technology	5.90 ***	6.27ª	5.74	5.82ª
Computers	4.05 ***	4.97	4.07 ***	4.80
Athletics & recreation	5.54	5.39	5.41	5.32
Beliefs & interests	5.94	5.60	5.75	5.69
Arts & literature	5.75ª ***	5.00	5.42ª **	4.84
Identity Prominence, Salience (scale: 0 – 7):				
Science & technology	3.94	3.85	4.03	4.04
Computers	2.47ª **	2.95ª	2.74ª *	3.20ª
Athletics & recreation	5.07ª	4.97	4.90ª	4.81
Beliefs & interests	4.34	4.23	4.45	4.41
Arts & literature	4.41ª **	3.99	4.24ª	3.96

Fig. 5.7: Example of results

(**Source:** based on review of literature)

Conclusions and Discussion

This section assesses how one's research findings relate to what the community of scholars knew already.

- You should summarize the most salient points of your research (tell the reader what you found out about your topic).
- Discuss the general significance of your topic and findings.
- You should discuss the shortcomings of your study and what implications these have for your findings.
- Discuss things future researchers should investigate about your topic.
- Leave the reader with the understanding he or she ought to have about the topic you spent so much time exploring.

REFERENCES

The references are just as important as any other part of your paper. They are the link to the community of scholars that will permit your reader to assess the worthiness of the claims you make in your paper. References also make the research process much more efficient because they make it very easy to look up sources of facts and ideas.

References Should be hanging indented, alphabetical on author's last name (by increasing year within same author) with information in order determined by type of source:

Article

Last Name, first name. Year. "Article title." *Journal Name* Volume: 1st Page-Last Page.

Lee, James Daniel. 2005. "Do Girls Change More than Boys? Gender Differences and Similarities in the Impact of New Relationships on Identities and Behaviors." *Self and Identity* 4:131-47.

Chapter

Last Name, first name. Year. "Chapter Name." Pages in the book in *Book Name*, edited by first name last name. City of Publisher: Publisher.

Book:

Last name, first name. Year. *Book Name*. City of Publisher: Publi

References

Should be hanging indented, alphabetical on author's last name (by increasing year within same author) with information in order determined by type of source:

A website:

Last Name (if available), first name. Year (if available). "Article or web page title." *Journal or Report Name* Volume (if available). http://address. Date accessed.

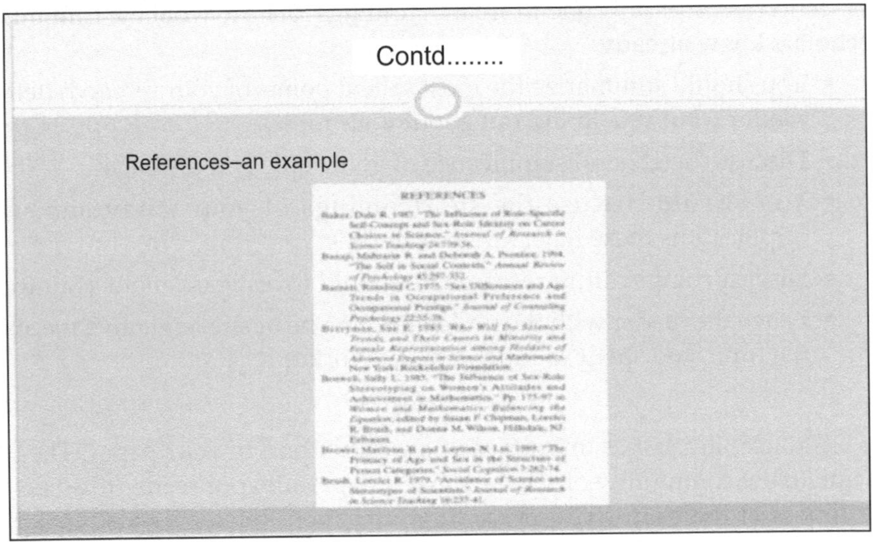

Fig. 5.8: Example of References

(**Source:** based on review of literature)

No Right Answer?

There is no right answer in a research paper—Just approximate representations of the truth that are closer or further away from that truth.

- The truth is:
  - From "Community of Scholars":

    What they said about your topic in the journals, books, and other publications

- From you:

  What your methods and analyses revealed about the topic.

PLAGIARISM

Finally...Avoiding Plagiarism

- What is it?
  - All knowledge in your head has either been copied from some place or originally discovered by you.
  - Most knowledge was copied.
  - This is true in most settings. General knowledge is copied. Most teachers' lectures are copied knowledge.
  - Humans are naturally copiers, but this is not what we would typically call "plagiarism."
  - Among other things, plagiarism refers to taking others' work and representing it as if it were your own.
  - To avoid plagiarism.
  - Document every source for information that is not "general knowledge"—this includes facts and ideas.
  - Cite every time a fact or idea is used unless it is clear that one citation is referring to a group of facts or ideas.
  - If you quote material, put quotation marks around the quoted stuff and include a page number within the citation.
  - It is alright to paraphrase material, but you still have to cite from where the paraphrased material came.
  - When in doubt, cite the source.
  - Improper citing is grounds for failure on the course paper.

Scientific Writing and Research Quality **Pages 48-63**
Edited by: Dr. Prasann Kumar & Dr. Pawan Kumar 'Bharti'
ISBN: 978-93-88854-48-1
Edition: 2020
Published by: Discovery Publishing House Pvt. Ltd., New Delhi (India)

6 Concept of 3I for Effective Research

Prasann Kumar[1,2]* & Shipa Rani Dey[1]

GRAPHICAL ABSTRACT

Keywords: *Concept, Data, Energy, Find, Gap*

Introduction

Difference in What?

Difference in subject matter (what questions are you researching?)

Difference in methods (how are you researching these questions?)

Difference in theories/theorizing (what are the answers to your questions?)

"Interesting" research is research that deviates from the mainstream: asks different questions, offers new ways of exploring these questions, and generates new perspectives or explanations about these questions.

1 Department of Agronomy, School of Agriculture, Lovely Professional University, Jalandhar, Punjab, India, 144411
2 Divison of Research and Development, Lovely Professional University, Jalandhar, Punjab, India, 144411

"What's new?"

Good Research Starts with Good RQs

Quiz: How can you find interesting research problems?

A. By asking your faculty advisor
B. By reading papers in the library
C. By observing practice
D. None of the above (suggest a better method)

Research Problems

- Where do we find good research problems?
  - By observing (something unexpected, paradoxical, or "different").
  - Observations that challenge common assumptions/expectations rather than affirm them.
  - "Gaps", anomalies, or paradoxes unresolved from prior research.
- What do we need to locate good research problems?
  - Superior observational skills.
  - Awareness of events around us.
  - Willingness to question everything.

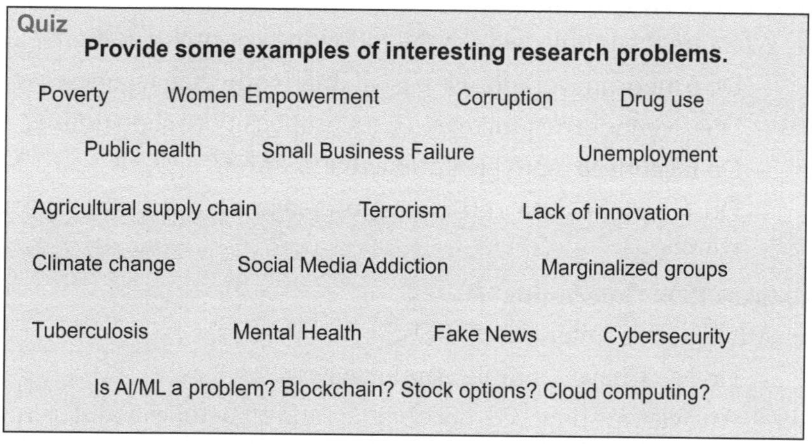

Fig. 6.1: Some examples of interesting research problem

(**Source:** based on review of literature)

The "Problem" of the Research Problem

- All problems are **NOT** equal:
  - Trivial problems have trivial solutions (stories).
  - Bigger, messier, complex problems may be hard to solve but are also more interesting and can generate useful insights.

- Research problems set the tone and direction for the rest of the research process.

Research Questions

- RQs are questions that we seek to answer about our research problems.
- Innovations:
  - What are the factors that drive innovation in firms?
  - What innovation strategy works best and under what circumstances?
  - Why do some innovations succeed and other innovations fail?
- Social media addiction:
  - What are the key drivers of social media addiction?
  - What intervention strategies can help mitigate social media addiction?
- Small business failure:
  - Why are failure rates so high among small businesses?
  - What policy interventions can best mitigate small business failures?
  - Which intervention will work best under economic upturns versus downturns?

Pointless Research Questions

- What are the problems with the following research questions?
  - Do American workers use e-mail differently than Japanese workers?
  - Does vendor trust increase one's propensity to shop online?
  - Do incentives motivate knowledge sharing?
  - Do frequent data refreshing increase data accuracy in a data warehouse?

What Makes RQs "Interesting"?

- Attributes of "interesting" RQs:
  - Do NOT have a simple yes/no answer.
  - Answers are nuanced, not obvious, and sometimes counter-intuitive.
  - Search for explanations, not just descriptions: "Why…", "How…", "Under what circumstances…"?
  - Appeal to a broad population.
  - Different.
- How to identify interesting RQs:
  - Requires deep knowledge of the problem domain (to see gaps/ problems).

- Requires time in the field talking to practitioners to understand their everyday problems.

Research Domain	Poor Research Questions	Good Research Questions
Trust in e-commerce	Does trust impact a person's propensity to buy Online?	What are the most effective ways for firms to build Online trust, given inherent barriers to Online trust formation such as anonymity, fraud, etc.?
Data warehousing	How is data accuracy in a warehouse related to the frequency of data refreshing?	How frequently should fact or dimension tables in a data warehouse be refreshed? What criteria/metrics can be used to determine that frequency?
Organizational change	Do IT users resist introduction of new IT?	How can firm managers motivate IT-driven change in a firm where employees have perpetually resisted change?
Incentives in knowledge management	How do incentives impact knowledge sharing among workers?	What incentives are most effective in promoting knowledge sharing and under what circumstances?

Fig. 6.2: Converting Poor RQ to Good RQ

(**Source:** based on review of literature)

The "Paradox" Approach

- Look for paradoxes (anomalies):
  - In the existing literature.
  - Between literature and observations.
  - Between expectations and observations.
- Examples:
  - If e-commerce was supposed to revitalize business, why did 90% of e-commerce firms go out of business?
  - Now that we have the best software engineering practices (e.g., CASE, CMM), why do 70% of large systems still fail today?
  - After spending millions on knowledge management initiatives, why do some firms still repeat prior mistakes, can't diffuse best practices, and don't learn?

More RP/RQ Examples from Current Projects

- Impact of healthcare IT in post-acute care settings:
  - How does healthcare IT impact readmissions, reimbursement, and clinical care in long-term and post-acute care facilities?

- Growth of adolescent drug use in India:
  - What are the key drivers of adolescent drug use in India?
  - What formal and informal interventions may help mitigate adolescent drug use in India?
- Information asymmetry in agricultural supply chains in India:
  - What are the sources and causes of information asymmetry in India's agricultural supply chains?
  - Do current practices help reduce this information asymmetry and are there better practices?
- Mental health care in India:
  - How can we destigmatize mental health care in India?
  - What mechanisms can help in the effective delivery of mental health care services in India?

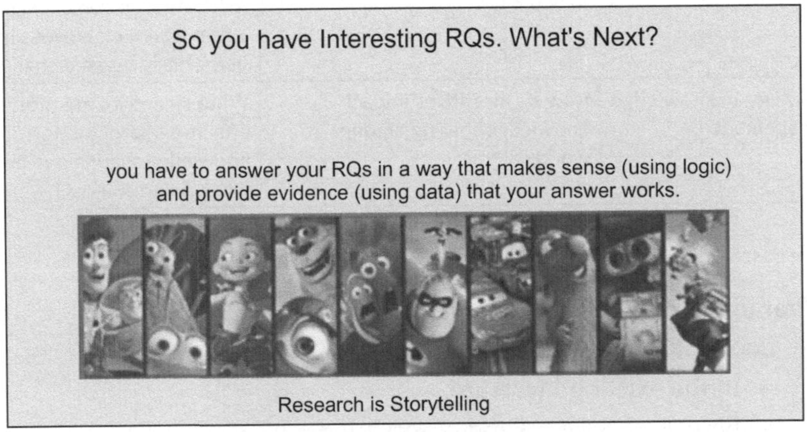

Fig. 6.3: Interesting RQ: What is next

(**Source:** based on review of literature)

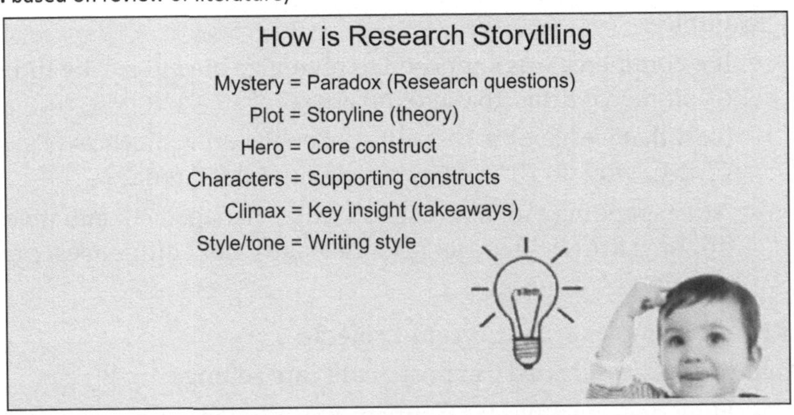

Fig. 6.4: what's make a great history

(**Source:** based on review of literature)

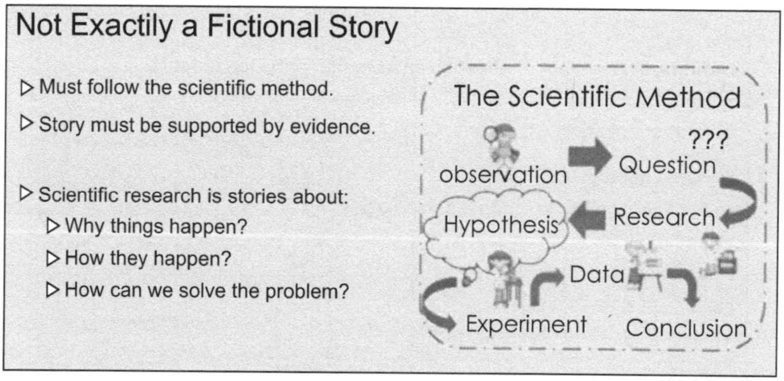

Fig. 6.5: Not Exactly a Fictional Story

(**Source:** based on review of literature)

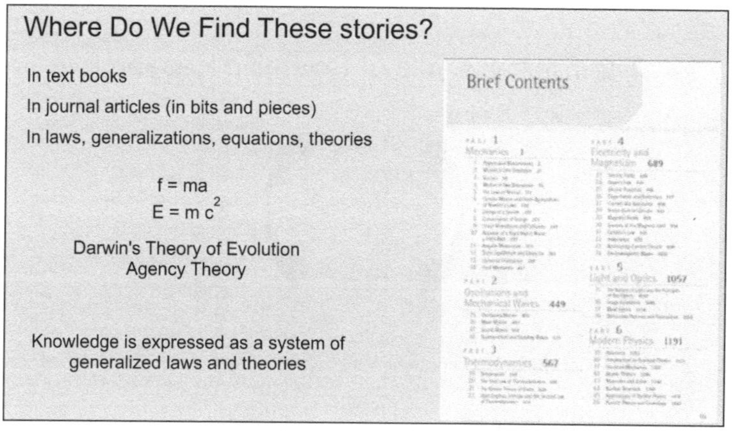

Fig. 6.6: Where do we find these stories?

(**Source:** based on review of literature)

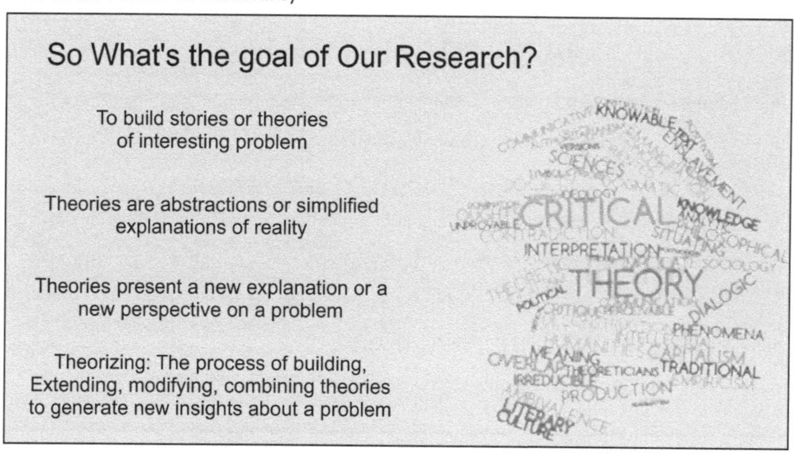

Fig. 6.7: So what's the Goal of Our Research?

(**Source:** based on review of literature)

Definition: A system of generalized laws that provides reasonable explanations of observed phenomena

What theory is not:

Conjectures/hunches
Lists of constructs, taxonomies, typologies
Hypotheses
Prior findings
Results of data analysis
Models (e.g., predictive models)
Reality

Fig. 6.8: What is a theory

(**Source:** based on review of literature)

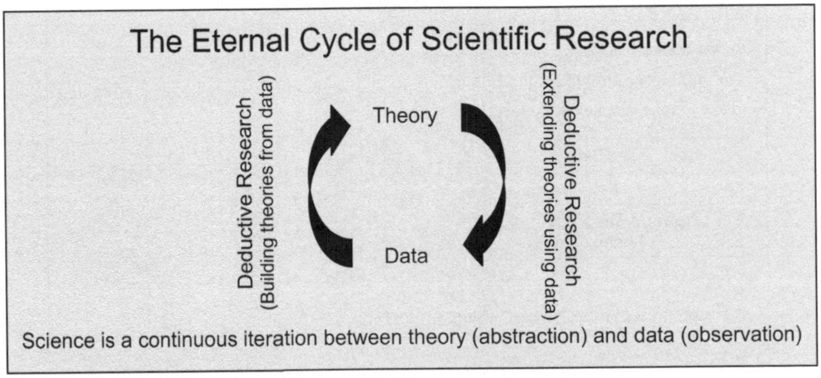

Fig. 6.9: The Eternal Cycle of Scientific Research

(**Source:** based on review of literature)

Why Should we Use Theories

- Theories embody our current state of knowledge about a certain phenomenon.
  - They synthesize prior empirical findings.
  - They help identify key factors, underlying processes, etc.
- Theories aid in sense-making:
  - They make sense of observed patterns by explaining these patterns.
  - They help bridge gaps in observations and/or other theories.
- Theories provide guidance for future research:
  - They identify constructs to measure and relationships to test.

Fig. 6.10: Why should we use theories

(**Source:** based on review of literature)

- Are all theories good?
    - All theories are NOT equal; some are trivial and pointless and some are simply wrong.
    - Good theories explain a phenomenon better than bad theories.
    - Good theories have useful practical implications.
    - Scientific research is a process of weeding out bad theories from good.
- How do we know which theories are good?
    - They must make sense (epical).
    - They must be supported by evidence (validation).
    - They must be independently testable (falsifiability).
    - They must be simple (parsimony).
    - They must apply across different contexts (generalizability).

Fig. 6.11: Goodness of Theories

(**Source:** based on review of literature)

Limits and Use of Theories

- Limits:
    - Theones are simplistic and tentative explanations of reality.
    - Theones are generalized explanations; may not explain specific situations i
    - Theones are sometimes wrong (i.e.. they don't fit evidence) and must be discarded.
    - Theones may limit our world view and cause us to miss important aspects of a research problem.
- How should be use theories:
    - Contextualize, extend, modify theories (not just use them as-is)
    - Consider using multiple theories if they provide a richer explanation than a single theory.
    - Consider using different theories across boundary conditions.
    - Test and weed out of poor theones.

Fig. 6.12: Limits and Use of theories

(**Source:** based on review of literature)

Theoretical Consideration

- Appropriateness of theory:
  - Can a chosen theory provide the best (most comprehensive) answer to your research questions,' or are there better theories?
  - If prior research have used one theory heavily and some research questions remained
  - unresolved, perhaps we need a different theory.
  - Did you capture most of the important constructs and relationships in your theory faithfully and accurately?
- One or more theories?
  - If each theory offer partial explanations; multiple theories may help.
  - Too many theories may mean no coherent theory ("theoretical promiscuity").
  - How many is too many: More than three.
  - If using multiple theories, try dissimilar theories from different referent disciplines to maximize explanatory power.

Fig. 6.13: Theoretical Considerations

(**Source:** based on review of literature)

Questions About Theories

- Can't we do research without theories?
  - Theory tells us which construct to measure and which associations to test.
  - If you have no idea what you should look for, there is a good chance that you may not find anything useful or insightful.
  - Without theory/logic, associations between variables are often spurious.
  - Arbitrary data collection and mindless data analysis are NOT research.
- Can we build theories from data?
  - We can, but only if empirical evidence is by logic.
  - Good theories require an engaging narrative and should provide actionable insights.

"Theory without practice is sterile; practice without theory is blind"- Kurt Lewin

Fig. 6.14: Questions about Theories

(**Source:** based on review of literature)

Components of a Theory

- Constructs:
  - Abstract concepts chosen specifically to explain a problem
  - May represent steady states or temporal tendencies (trust, learning).
  - Should be defined at the right level of analysis:
  - Individual learning is different from organizational teaming.
- Variables are measurable representations of constructs:
  - IQ score is a measure of intelligence
  - Some constructs (age. firm size) are easy to measure and others are hard (creativity, prejudice).
  - Constructs conceptuaized at the theoretical level; variables are operationalized and measured at the empirical level.

Fig. 6.15: Components of a theory

(**Source:** based on review of literature)

Components of a Theory

- Propositions:
  - Associations between constructs that we want to test
  - Stated in a declarative and causal form.
    - Example: Children's intelligence has a positive effect on their academic learning.
  - Derived based on deductive logic (not observed evidence)
    - Tested using empirical evidence.
  - May be conjectural but MUST be testable (falsifiable).

Fig. 6.16: Continuation of figure 15

(**Source:** based on review of literature)

Components of a Theory

- Logic:
  - The "glue" that ties constructs into propositions.
- Assumption/Boundary Conditions:
  - Defines when a theory works and when it does not.
    - Examples: Rational versus political choice, individualistic versus collectivist
    - cultures, early versus later stages of human behavior.
  - Different theories may be needed across boundary conditions.

Fig. 6.17: Continuation of figure 16

(**Source:** based on review of literature)

Agency Theory

- Phenomenon: Two-pary relationship with goal conflict (employe-employee, buyer-seller).
- Objective: To specify optimal contracts and conditions under which such contracts can minimize goal conflict.

  Assumptions. People are self-interested, boundedly rational, risk-averse.

  Storyline:
  - Principal P employs agent A to perform certain tasks on its behalf., but A has different goats than P.
  - Information asymmetry problems:
    - Moral hazard: A does not put forth needed effort because P can t observe its behavior.
    - Adverse selection A misrepresents its expertise to get the job because P can't test its skills.
  - Contracts: Behavior-based (A's choice), outcome-based (P's choice), mixed.
  - Tools to improve the efficacy of behavior-based contracts:
    - Monitoring mechanisms (to counter moral hazard).
    - Renewable contracts contingent on A's performance
    - Improving task programmability.

Fig. 6.18: Agency Theory

(**Source:** based on review of literature)

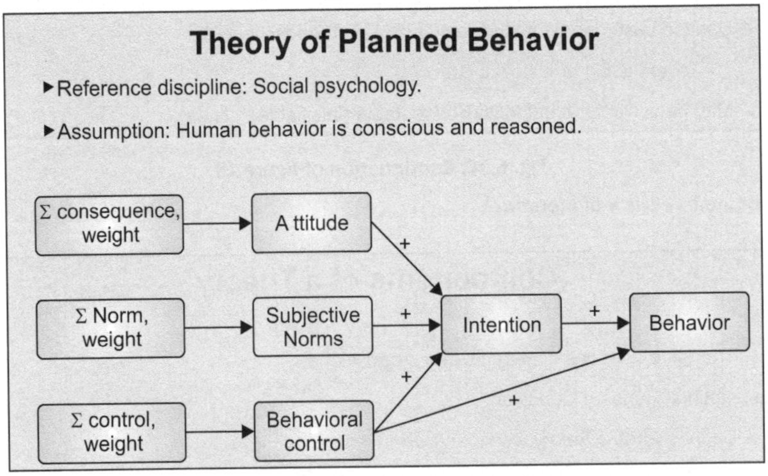

Fig. 6.19: Theory of planned behaviour

(**Source:** based on review of literature)

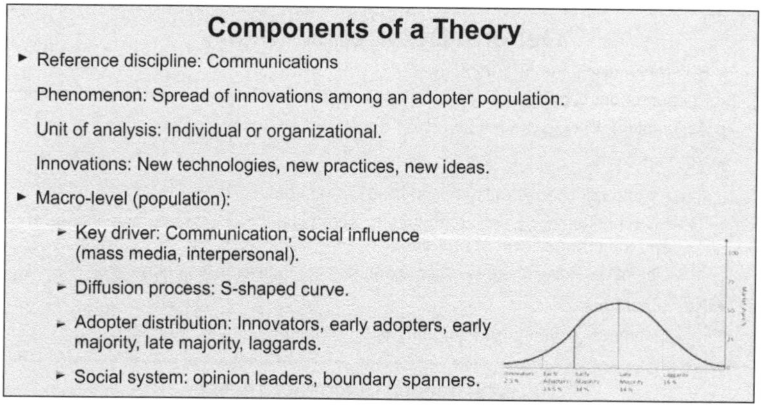

Fig. 6.20: Innovation Diffusion Theory

(**Source:** based on review of literature)

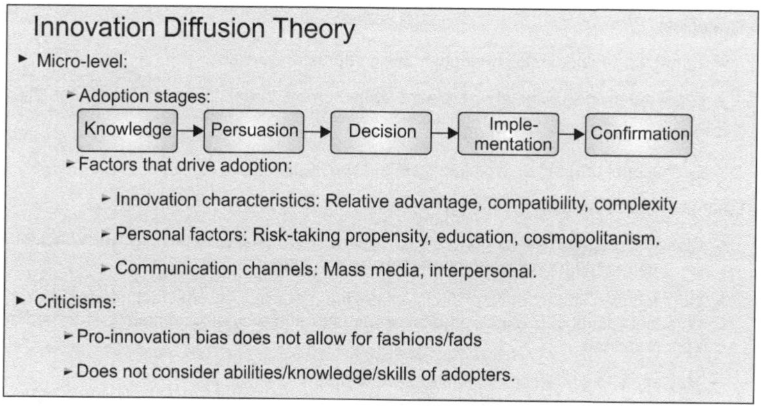

Fig. 6.21: Continuation of figure 20

(**Source:** based on review of literature)

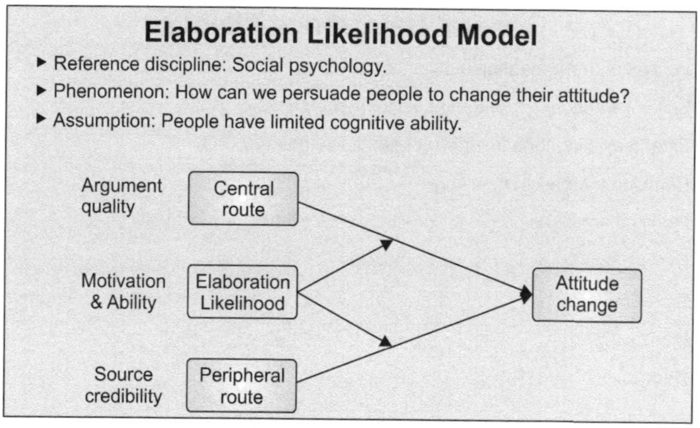

Fig. 6.22: Continuation of figure 21

(**Source:** based on review of literature)

General Deterrence Theory

- Reference discipline: Criminology.
- Phenomenon: Why do non-deviant people sometimes engage in deviant behaviors?
- Assumption: People are rational (cost-benefit).
- Core precepts:
  - People will choose utility-maximizing deviant behaviors.
  - Such behaviors can be controlled by increasing their cost (e.g., punishement) and the probability of apprehension.
  - Objective: Prevent crimes bu making criminal activities less attractive.
- Key constructs:
  - Swiftness, severity, and certainty of punishments.

Fig. 6.23: General Deterrence Theory

(**Source:** based on review of literature)

General Deterrence Theory

- Strategies:
  - Target hardening: install deadbolts. build self-defense skills.
  - Legal deterrents: eliminate parole for some crimes, three strikes law. death penalty.
  - Increased chances of apprehension: neighborhood watch programs.
  - Educational programs: prominently displayed legal notices.
- Difference from classical criminology research:
  - Classical research seeks generalized causes of criminal behaviors (poverty, lack of education), and rehabilitative strategies for criminals.
  - GOT focuses on the criminal decision making process, personal factors (criminal's personal values, affluence), situational factors (efficiency of local police, likelihood of apprehension).
  - May apply to contemporary white-collar crimes.

Fig. 6.24: Continuation of figure 23

(**Source:** based on review of literature)

General Deterrence Theory

- The process of using theories in scientific research:
  - Build new theories through inductive research
  - Extend existing theories through deductive research.
  - Combine theories in new ways
  - Modify theories designed for one context for a different context.
  - Explore boundary conditions of theories
- Two approaches:
  - Inductive.
  - Deductive.
  - Abductive.

Fig. 6.25: Theorizing

(**Source:** based on review of literature)

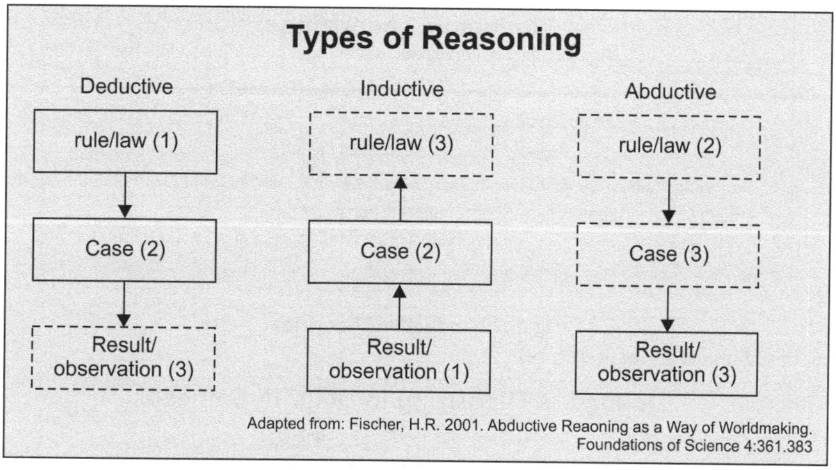

Fig. 6.26: Types of Reasoning

(**Source:** based on review of literature)

Deduction, Induction and Abduction

Deductive	Inductive	Abductive
All men are mortal;	Socrates is a man;	All men are mortal;
Socrates is a man;	Socrates is a mortal;	Socrates is a mortal;
Socrates is mortal.	All men are mortal;	Socrates is a man.

Adapted from: Mul. J. Castrum t. and T. Deacon 2008. Double Description. What is it' How Does it work' What Do we learn's is j. Hoffmeyer (ed) A legacy for Living Systems Gregory Bateson As Precursor to Biosermiotics.

Always true — May not be true

Fig. 6.27: Deduction, Induction and Abduction

(**Source:** based on review of literature)

Deductive Theorizing

- Extend/modify existing theories to explain a new context:
  - Extend individual learning theories to explain organizational learning.
  - Leverages our current inventory of social science theories.
  - Efficient way of building new theories.
- Apply existing theories in entirely new contexts by drawing upon the structural similarities between the two contexts:
  - Extending theories using reasoning by analogy.
  - Example Markus (1987)'s critical mass theory of network growth.

Fig. 6.28: Deductive Theorizing

(**Source:** based on review of literature)

Inductive Theorizing

- Build theories based on observed patterns:
  - Inspired by qualitative methods like ethnography and grounded theory.
  - Patterns may be observed by grouping predictors:
    - Individual, organizational, and technological factors.
  - Requires experienced researchers to reduce biases in interpretations.
  - Patterns must be explained conceptually to constitute theory.
- Far more potent approach to building theories than deductive but also more error-prone.
- Inductive patterns may require deductive testing to prove that the theory works.

Fig. 6.29: Inductive Theorizing

(**Source:** based on review of literature)

Deductive Theorizing to Build Hypotheses

- Knowledge Transfer in Intraorganizational Networks (Tsai 2001):
  - Integrated social network effects with absorptive capacity.
  - H1 The centrality of an organizational unit's network position is positively related to its innovation
  - H2. An organizational unit's absorptive capacity is positively related to its innovation.
  - H3 The centrality of an organizational unit's network position is more positively related to its innovation when the unit has higher absorptive capacity than when it has lower absorptive capacity.

Source Tsai. W, "Knowledge Transfer in Intraorganizational Networks Effects of Network Position and Absorptive Capacity on Business Unit Innovator! and Performance." Academy of Management Journal (44:5). 2001.996-1004.

Fig. 6.30: Deductive Theorizing to Build Hypothesis

(**Source:** based on review of literature)

Deductive Theorizing of Build Hypotheses

- Exploration versus Exploitation: Firm Ambidexterity Effects (He & Wong 2004):
  - Exploring the tension between two contrasting innovation strategies.
  - Exploration
    - Focus on designing new products, extending product range, etc
    - Characterized by search, discovery, experimentation. risk taking, organic structures, autonomy, etc
  - Exploitation:
    - Focus on improving quality of existing products, reducing costs, etc.
    - Characterized by efficiency, using tried and tested processes, avoiding risks, mechanistic structures, etc,
  - H1 There is a positive interaction effect between exploration and exploitation innovation strategies on firm performance
  - H2 The relative imbalance (absolute difference) between exploration and exploitation strategies is negatively related to firm performance.

Source: He. Z.L and Wong. P.K.. "Exploration vs. Exploitation: An Empirical Test of the Ambidexterity Hypothesis." Organization Science (15:4), 2004,481-494

Fig. 6.31: Continuation of figure 30

(**Source:** based on review of literature)

Deductive Theorizing of Build Hypotheses

- What drives unethical behaviors: Contagion or differentiation (Gino et al. 2009):
    - Comparing three theories:
    - Rational crime theory.
    - Norm-focus theory.
    - Social identity theory.

Source: Gino F. Ayad. S. and Artery. D.. '**Contagion** and Differentiation in Unethical Behavior The Effect of One Bad Apple **on (he** Barrel.' Psychological Science **(20:3). 2009.**393-398.

Fig. 6.32: Continuation of figure 31

(**Source:** based on review of literature)

REFERENCES

Bhattacharjee A. 2019. Professor of ISDS, Exide Professor of Business Ethics, University of South Florida, Tampa, USA.

Scientific Writing and Research Quality
Edited by: Dr. Prasann Kumar & Dr. Pawan Kumar 'Bharti'
ISBN: 978-93-88854-48-1
Edition: 2020
Published by: Discovery Publishing House Pvt. Ltd., New Delhi (India)

Pages 64-68

7

How to Write a Winning Grant Proposal

Prasann Kumar[1,2]* & Shipa Rani Dey[1]

GRAPHICAL ABSTRACT

Keywords: Agronomy, Board, Coin, Fund, Grant, Proposal, Writing

Introduction

Why This Topic?

- Research budgets are shrinking everywhere.
- Researchers are being forced to seek external funding.
- But writing a good research grant proposal is challenging.

To help you gain insight into the way decision-makers assess and evaluate research proposals.

Grants: *Some Basics*

- Grants are sums of money awarded to finance particular activities and not to be paid back - but to deliver a product/solution!

1 Department of Agronomy, School of Agriculture, Lovely Professional University, Jalandhar, Punjab, India, 144411
2 Divison of Research and Development, Lovely Professional University, Jalandhar, Punjab, India, 144411

- It is important to understand the goals of the funding bodies and their grant programs...
- Allows better planning
- Decisions are made on the applicant's ability to tune the proposed research activities to the interests of the funding body.

Before beginning to prepare a grant proposal, consider the following:

- Rule #1: Believe that someone wants to give you the money.
- Consider the long-term goals of your institution.
- Start with the end in mind (top down approach).
- Identify yourself and your strengths.
- Create a comprehensive plan - not just a proposal of what you wish to achieve.

Do Your Homework

- Research prospective funding bodies.

  e.g. DST, DBT, ICSSR etc.
- Target funding source that has interest in your organisation and programme.
- Collaborate with experts if funding is not available in your field.. Synergetic activities.
  - Give more and take less .. Develop that attitude

Make Contact with Funding Organisations

- Gather information on:
- Details of grants available.
- How to apply for them.
- Members of committees etc.

Seek Answers to the Following Questions

- What are the deadlines for submission?
- How long will the process take?
- What is the proper way to approach them?
- How many people apply each year and what percentage get grants?
- Most answers can be found on the funding body's website, research guide, annual report & future plans.

Some Points to Remember

- You and the funders are both professionals coming together for a specific purpose.

- Get to know relevant people in the funding body.
- Get help of finance office on matters relating to staff costs, travel, overheads etc.
- Seek professional advice on confidentiality, possible restrictions on publications, liabilities and disputes etc.

Approaching the Proposal

Always remember:

- Your case will be read by one or two experts in your field but others in the judgement panel won't be experts. *You must write for their benefit too.*
- Ask lots of people to help you ...improve your proposal.
- Make sure the first page acts as a *stand-alone* summary of the entire proposal.

Major Criteria: *Questions to be Answered*

- Do the proposers have a good idea on which to base their work?
- Does the proposal explain clearly what work will be done?
- Is there evidence that the proposers know about relevant work that others have done?
- Do the proposers have a good track record, both of doing good research and of publishing it?
- What are the implications for policy and practice? How will these be taken up?

Secondary Criteria

- An applicant with existing funding may be favoured due to evidence of a good track record.
- Also priority is given to new researchers in the field.
- Funders generally prefer to offer a reasonable balance of support for different research areas.
- Evidence of industrial interest in the proposal and its potential for future exploitation will count in favour.

Common Shortcomings

- It is not clear which research questions are being addressed by the proposal.
- The questions being addressed are ill-formed.
- It is not clear why the questions are worth addressing.
- The proposal is just a routine application of a known technique.
- Industry ought to be doing it instead.

Writing Grant Application - Formal Structure

Essential Contents:

- Statement of the problem.
- Summary of current developments in the field.
- Statement of what is new about the project.
- Indication of the extent to which the research builds on previous work by you and by others?

Methods: *Questions to be answered*

- What methods will be applied to achieve the aims? The methodology must be described in detail and clearly related to the research questions.
- Are the chosen methods sufficiently rigorous to produce clear answers?
- What is the timetable? This must be realistic.

Ethical Aspects

- Make sure your proposal addresses relevant ethical considerations.

Dissemination: Questions to be Answered

- What audience should be targeted to achieve the maximum impact?
- How might this audience best be reached?
- What is the budget for dissemination?

Personnel

- Explain the staffing requirements in detail and ensure that this make sense.
- It is essential to provide brief details of the relevant qualifications and experience of the staff.
- To minimise expenses, the plan should include the phasing out of staff whenever their tasks are completed.

Budget

- The application should include an itemised budget setting out the costs year by year.
- A cost justification for each item should be given.
- The budget should be exhaustive.
- If additional funding from other sources is sought then this should be made clear.

Timing

- The individual tasks should be sequentially given with realistic durations.

- Detailed reasoning should be given for the task sequence and durations.

Revising Your Proposal

- Seek regular feedback from readers as soon as possible during the development of the proposal, allowing time to receive responses.
- Bear in mind that strong grant proposals take a long time to develop, so plan well ahead to ensure meeting the deadline.

Some Advice

- Do not feel ashamed or embarrassed about asking for money or promoting yourself.
- If you never ask for the money, it will never be offered.
- If at first you don't succeed, try and try again.
- Learn from feedback regarding a rejected proposal.
- Be positive!

REFERENCES

https://ums.lpu.in/lpuums/frmResearchPanelsView.aspx

Scientific Writing and Research Quality
Edited by: Dr. Prasann Kumar & Dr. Pawan Kumar 'Bharti'
ISBN: 978-93-88854-48-1
Edition: 2020
Published by: Discovery Publishing House Pvt. Ltd., New Delhi (India)

Pages 69-78

8

Intellectual Property Rights
An Overview

Prasann Kumar[1,2]* & Shipa Rani Dey[1]

GRAPHICAL ABSTRACT

Keywords: *Intellectual, Property, Rights*

Introduction

- Exclusive rights for creation of mind
- Given for Intangible assets
- Can be given for an Idea
- Rights which can abstain others from using their assets
- Territorial rights
- Negative rights
- Given in both scientific as well as artistic fields

1 Department of Agronomy, School of Agriculture, Lovely Professional University, Jalandhar, Punjab, India, 144411

2 Divison of Research and Development, Lovely Professional University, Jalandhar, Punjab, India, 144411

Property VS. Intellectual rights

Real Property

- Own and Use
- Sell
- Rent
- Tangible

Intellectual Right

- Own and Use
- Sell
- Licence
- Sue
- Intangible

Types of Intellectual Property

Industrial property

- Patents
- Trademarks
- Trade dress
- Trade secret
- Industrial designs
- Geographical Indications
- Plant Breeders Rights

Artistic

- Copyrights
- The following Acts are being followed in India for IPR:
  - The Patents Act 1970 (as amended)
  - The Copyright Act 1957 (as amended)
  - The Trade Marks Act 1999
  - The Designs Act 2001
  - The Geographical Indications of Goods (Registrations and Protection) Act, 1999
  - The Semiconductor Integrated circuit Layout-Design Act 2000
  - The Protection of Plant Varieties and Farmers Rights Act 2001
  - The Biological Diversity Act 2002

World intellectual property organization

- Created in 1967 to encourage creative activity and to promote intellectual property throughout the world
- Came into force in 1970
- Amended on Sep 28 1979, modified on 3 Feb 1984, 3 Oct 2001
- Headquarters in Geneva Switzerland
- 187 member states, 26 international treaties
- Predecessor was BIRPI (*Bureaux InternationauxRéunis pour la Protection de la PropriétéIntellectuelle)*
- Mission is to promote through international cooperation the creation, dissemination use and protection of works of the human mind for the economic, cultural and social progress of all mankind.

The international patent system PCT

- Came into existence in 1978.
- The patent cooperation treaty is the international system for filing, searching and examination of patents.
- By filing one international patent application one can seek patent protection in 148 countries.
- No provision of this treaty shall diminish the rights of Paris convention.
- One international application is filed by a member country and within 12 months of this application one can file complete application.
- After 18 months the international search report is published.
- After 30 months the PCT goes in national phase entry of different countries.
- After entering the national phase each member country treats the patent according to its own state laws.

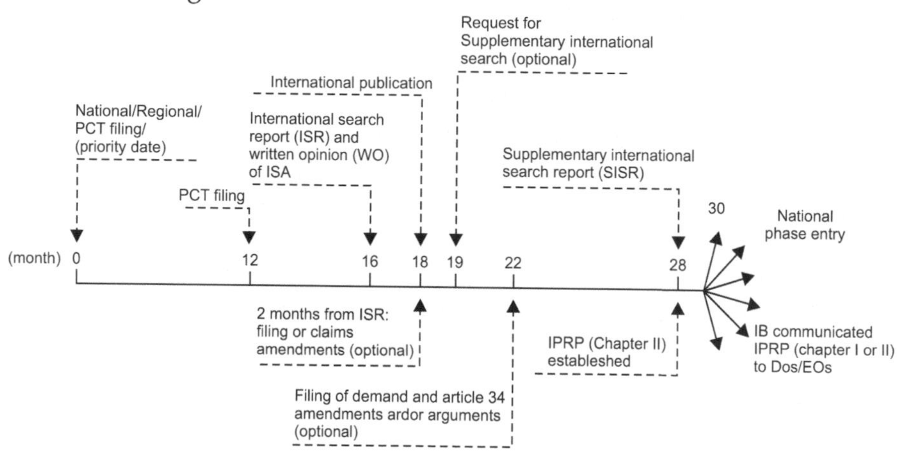

Fig. 8.1: PCT Timeline

(**Source:** based on review of literature)

Copyrights

Literary and artistic works

- literary works such as novels, poems, plays, reference works, newspaper articles;
- computer programs, databases;
- films, musical compositions, and choreography;
- artistic works such as paintings, drawings, photographs, and sculpture;
- architecture
- advertisements, maps, and technical drawings
- **economic rights**, which allow the rights owner to derive financial reward from the use of his works by others
- **moral rights**, which protect the non-economic interests of the author.
- The economic rights owner of a work can prohibit or authorize:
- its reproduction in various forms, such as printed publication or sound recording;
- its public performance, such as in a play or musical work;
- its recording, for example, in the form of compact discs or DVDs;
- its broadcasting, by radio, cable or satellite;
- its translation into other languages; and
- its adaptation, such as a novel into a film screenplay.

Steps to copyright

- Create
- Register Your Copyright
  - www.copyright.gov.in
  - Can be done electronically
- Send the Package to the Copyright Office
  - May not be necessary if you register online

Copyright term

- Literary work: 60 years after the death of the author
- Cinematographic work: 60 years from first showing
- Photographic work: 25 years from the year photograph was created
- Broadcasting rights: 25 years
- Criminal offence
- Fine from ₹ 20,000 to 3,00,000 and imprisonment from 6 months to 3 years

Trademark

Word, phrase, symbol, sign, design and expression which identifies a product or services

Term of trademark is 10 years and can be renewed after that

Fig. 8.2: Trademark Examples

(**Source:** based on review of literature)

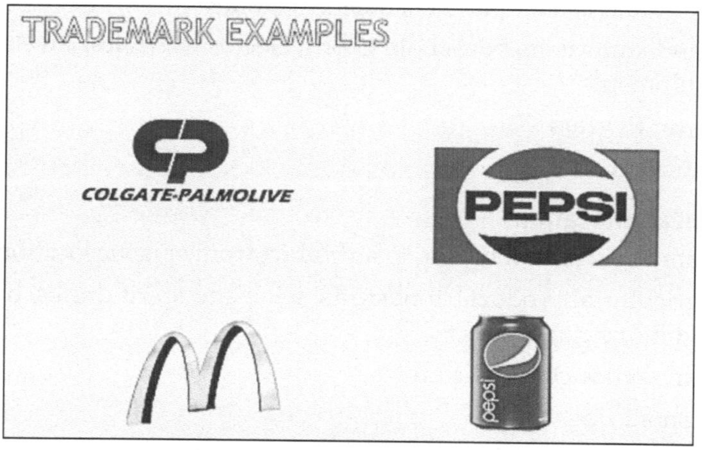

Fig. 8.3: Continuation of figure 2

(**Source:** based on review of literature)

Fig. 8.4: Continuation of figure 3

(**Source:** based on review of literature)

Trade Dress

- Visual appearance and packaging of product
- Anything that creates the overall look and feel of a brand in the marketplace could be a trade dress.
- Consumer really believes that the trade dress is a source indicator of distinguishing the goods and services of one from those of others.
- The configuration of shapes, designs, colors, or materials that make up the trade dress in question must not serve a utility or function outside of creating recognition in the consumer's mind.
- The statutory requirement for the registration of trade dress is same as that of the registration is word/ logo mark.

Industrial Designs/Design Patent

- Ornamental or aesthetic aspect of an article
- Three dimensional- shape of the article
- Two dimensional-patterns, lines or colours
- Handicrafts item, household goods, electronic device, jewelry, lighting equipment
- Term: 15 years
- Renewed after 10 years

Geographical Indications

- Name or sign that belong to a product from specific location
- Agricultural products, foodstuffs, wine and spirit drinks, handicrafts, and industrial products.
- Some product in India are:
- Basmati rice
- Darjeeling tea
- Mysore silk
- Kota doria
- Term: 10 years with renewal time to time

Trade Secret

- Formula, practice, process, design, instrument, pattern, commercial method, or compilation of information
- No public disclosure required
- Last for long
- But yes chances of leakage are there through reverse engineering
- Coca Cola

- Green Chartreuse liqueur protected by confidential information of the ingredients

Utility Models

- The requirements for acquiring a utility model are less stringent than for patents.
- The term of protection for utility models is shorter than for patents and varies from country to country (usually between 7 and 10 years without the possibility of extension or renewal).
- Utility models are much cheaper to obtain and to maintain
- In some countries, utility model protection can only be obtained for certain fields of technology and only for products but not for processes
- India does not have provision for utility models

Protection of Plant Variety and Farmers Act

- To establish an effective system for the protection of plant varieties, the rights of farmers and plant breeders and to encourage the development of new varieties of plants.
- To recognize and protect the rights of farmers in respect of their contributions made at any time in conserving, improving and making available plant genetic resources for the development of new plant varieties.
- To accelerate agricultural development in the country, protect plant breeders' rights; stimulate investment for research and development both in public & private sector for the development of new plant varieties.
- Facilitate the growth of seed industry in the country which will ensure the availability of high quality seeds and planting material to the farmers.

Farmers Variety

- Has been traditionally cultivated, evolved by farmers, have common knowledge.

Extant Variety

- (*i*) notified under section 5 of the Seeds Act, 1966 (54 of 1966); or (*ii*) a farmers' variety; or (*iii*) a variety about which there is common knowledge; or (iv) any other variety which is in the public domain.

Essentially Derived

- derived from another variety (protected or otherwise) able to transfer to the progeny

- **(A) Novelty**–Plant variety is novel if at the date of filing of the application for registration for protection, the propagating or harvested material of such variety has not been sold or otherwise disposed of by or with the consent of breeder or his successor for the purpose of exploitation of such variety- (*i*) in India earlier than one year or (*ii*) outside India , in the case of trees or vines earlier than six years or in any other case, earlier than four years, before the date of filing such application: Provided that a trial of a new variety which has not been sold otherwise disposed of shall not affect the right to protection. Provided further that the fact that on the date of filing the application for registration, propagating or harvested material of such variety has become a matter of common knowledge other than through the aforesaid manner shall not affect the criteria of novelty for such variety.
- **(B) Distinctiveness:** New plant variety will be considered distinct if it is clearly distinguishable by at least one essential characteristic from any other variety whose existence is a matter of common knowledge in any country at the time of filing of the application.

  (C) Uniformity: New plant variety will pass uniformity test, if subject to the variation that may be expected from the particular features of its propagation, it is sufficiently uniform in its essential characteristics.

  (D) Stability: New plant variety will be considered stable if its essential characteristics remain unchanged after repeated propagation or, in the case of a particular cycle of propagation, at the end of each such cycle.

Compulsory Plant Variety Denomination

After satisfying the above four essential criteria every applicant shall assign a single and distinct denomination to a variety with respect to which he is seeking registration.

Cannot be Protected

A plant variety which is :

(*i*) not capable of identifying such variety; or

(*ii*) consists solely of figures; or

(*iii*) is liable to mislead or to cause confusion concerning the characteristics, value, identify of such variety, or the identity of breeder of such variety;

(*iv*) is likely to deceive the public or cause confusion in the public regarding the identity of such variety;

(*v*) is comprised of nay matter likely to hurt the religious sentiments respectively of any class or section of the citizens of India;

(*vi*) is prohibited for use as a name or emblem for any of the purposes;

(*vii*) is comprised of solely or partly of geographical name.

Term of Protection

(*i*) In the case of trees and vines, eighteen years from the date of registration of the variety;

(*ii*) In the case of extant varieties, fifteen years from the date of the notification of that variety by the Central Government under section 5 of the Seeds Act, 1966

(*iii*) In the other cases, fifteen years from the date of registration of the variety. Initially the certificate of registration shall be valid for nine years in the case of trees and vines and six years in the case of other crops and may be revived and renewed for the remaining period on payment of fees as may be fixed by the rules.

Case Studies

IN244542: Indian Council of Agricultural Research

1. The polymeric seed coats characterized in that a polymer matrix comprising either of alkyl acrylates; polyethylene glycols and derivatives; polyvinylpyrrolidones; polyvinyl chlorides; cellulose or starch or their derivatives, wood rosin, gums or the likes, or mixtures of either two or more polymers, derivatives of polymers, polymer clay adducts or their combinations is employed, without or with 0.01 to 10 percent of a biopesticide incorporated in the matrix by dry blending or employing polar or / and non-polar solvents or blends of polar / non-polar solvents and a need based addition of 0.05 to 10 percent of surfactants to obtain a homogeneous powder or slurry , providing seed coats at 0.1 to 5 percent (seed basis) of the polymer alone or the polymer containing monolithically dispersed 0.01 to 10 percent of the bioactive ingredient for situation specific sustenance of seed quality or active ingredient release.
2. **IN237012: Harbhanjan Singh Sandhu:** The invention provides for an improved agriculture harrow disk comprising: a metal base disk; a plurality of metallic segments connected to the said base disk at its periphery to form the harrow disk of required diameter; the number and size of said metallic segments vary as per the required diameter of harrow disk. On wear and tear the segments can be replaced without wasting the entire harrow disk.
   - **IN242829: CSK Himachal Pradesh Krishi Vishwavidyalaya**
   - This invention relates to a process for preparation of citrus based slurry use to control insects, pest in agriculture and organic farming comprising of Preparing citrus slurry by air drying citrus waste including peel, seed left over pulp after extracting juice from selected fruits, again drying at 30°C for 12 hours, grindings, sieving through

O-size mesh, to obtain citrus powder, Said powder is mixed with petroleum ether in the ratio of 1:20 and subjected the same to heating at 40-65°C in soxhlet apparatus, recycling the condensed vapours, continuing heating for 15 to 25 cycles obtaining extract containing citrus fruits extract and petroleum ether, subjecting the extract to flash evaporation under vacuum at 25-30°C to obtain the slurry, Optionally converting said slurry into Emulsifiable Concentrate, dust or organic manure form.

- **IN208950: Makhteshim Chemical Works Ltd.**
- A sheet for pest control, wherein said sheet is of polymeric material and comprises at least two layers; a top layer and a bottom layer, wherein the bottom layer contains a herbicide and one or more pesticides selected from among fungicides and insecticides, and the top layer optionally containing an insecticide and/or fungicide. Other aspects of the invention include a polymeric composition used in the preparation of the sheets and a method for pest control in agriculture, horticulture and gardens.

Conclusion

Intellectual property (IP) is a category of property that includes intangible creations of the human intellect. The most prominent types of intellectual property are copyrights, patents, and trademarks, though many other types also exist, and some countries recognize more types than others. It was not until the 19th century that the term "intellectual property" began to be used, and not until the late 20th century that it became commonplace in the majority of the world. The main purpose of intellectual property law is to encourage the creation of a wide variety of intellectual goods. To achieve this, the law gives people and businesses property rights to the information and intellectual goods they create, usually for a limited period of time. This gives economic incentive for their creation, because it allows people to profit from the information and intellectual goods they create. These economic incentives are expected to stimulate innovation and contribute to the technological progress of countries, which depends on the extent of protection granted to innovators.

REFERENCES

https://www.itu.int/en/ITU-T/ipr/Pages/default.aspx

www.ipindia.nic.in/

https://en.wikipedia.org/wiki/Intellectual_property

Scientific Writing and Research Quality
Edited by: Dr. Prasann Kumar & Dr. Pawan Kumar 'Bharti'
ISBN: 978-93-88854-48-1
Edition: 2020
Published by: Discovery Publishing House Pvt. Ltd., New Delhi (India)

Pages 79-86

9

Plagiarism in Research

Prasann Kumar[1,2]* & Shipa Rani Dey[1]

GRAPHICAL ABSTRACT

Introduction

Find someone...

1. Who can play guitar ______________.
2. Find someone who knows a person who can download torrent movies __________.
3. Find someone who has never taught plagiarism ________________.
4. Find someone who knows a person whose research was rejected because of plagiarism ______________.
5. Find someone who can dance very well ________________.

[1] Department of Agronomy, School of Agriculture, Lovely Professional University, Jalandhar, Punjab, India, 144411

[2] Divison of Research and Development, Lovely Professional University, Jalandhar, Punjab, India, 144411

6. Who knows a student who plagiarized in class assignment ________________.
7. Whose student has never plagiarized ______________________.
8. Find someone who has been taught plagiarism in undergrad or postgrad __________.
9. Find someone who supports plagiarism in assignment but not in research ___________.
10. Find someone who copied and forgot to cite the source ________________________.

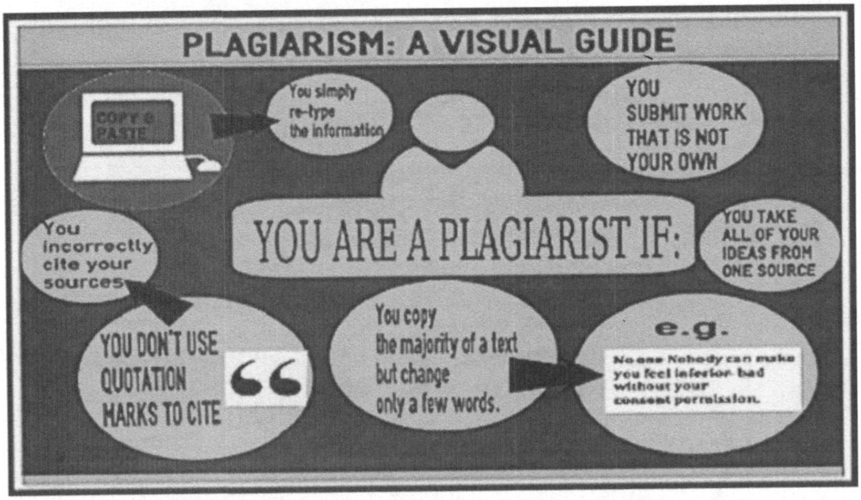

Fig. 9.1: What is plagiarism? And what is not?

(**Source:** based on review of literature)

To reinstate our knowledge of Plagiarism and to explore certain misconceptions about Plagiarism.

Ques 1. Sam can copy from an encyclopaedia without citing the source because this information is considered common knowledge.

Ques 2. Sue researches and takes notes in her own words. Later, when typing her essay, she does not give credit to the author because they are not the author's exact words. She is plagiarising her research.

Ques 3. Joey is good at taking test, but does not write papers very well. He does a lot of research, decides to rely heavily on quotations and does an exemplary job of citing his sources. Is this plagiarism?

Ques 4. Greg uses information from his Geology lab workbook in his lab report. Does he need to cite it?

Ques 5. Patrick took a paper he wrote for his Education class and handed in the same paper for his Psychology class. This is considered plagiarism.

Citation

Ques. 1. Tara can use an article in an online database without criting it if:

A. It only contains information found in other articles
B. She only uses the abstract
C. She can never do this
D. It was used in class discussion

Fig. 9.2: Tara can use an article in an online database without citing it if:

(**Source:** based on review of literature)

Ques. 2. Which is not a benefits of citing your sources:

A. Avoids plagiarism
B. Adds credibility
C. Avoids job loss
D. Helps reader find your sources

Fig. 9.3: Which is not a benefits of citing your sources

(**Source:** based on review of literature)

Ques. 3. Eric found an article online for his PPT which addresses issues he has been discussing in class. How can he responsibly include a direct quote from this article in his presentation?

A. A parenthetical citation on that particular slide
B. A citation on a works cited slide
C. Both A and B
D. Formal Citations are not needed for PPTs

Fig. 9.4: Question number 3

(**Source:** based on review of literature)

Ques. 4. Ruby wants to include a diagram of the reproduction cycle in her biology term paper. How can she responsible do this?

A. An in-text parenthetical Citation

B. A full citation in a bibliography

C. Both A and B

D. Formal citations are not needed for diagrams and images.

Fig. 9.5: Question number 4

(**Source:** based on review of literature)

Ques. 5. If Jessica got information from multiple articles that cover similar information, she

A. Must always cite all the sources

B. Only needs to cite one source, it doesn't matter which one.

C. Only needs to cite the sources which contained the most information, but adds more credibility

D. Doesn't need to cite any material since it is common knowledge

Fig. 9.6: Question number 5

(**Source:** based on review of literature)

Ques. 1. Mary wrote a paper in first year composition which she could now use in her second year sociology course. She should

A. Use it but change a few words

B. Use it because it has been already been given high credits

C. Discuss it's use with her professor

D. Use it because she is the original author

Fig. 9.7: Mary wrote a paper in first year composition

(**Source:** based on review of literature)

Ques. 2. How can Shushma use information from an un-copyrighted internet source such as Wikipedia?

A. Not copyrighted can use anyway she wants
B. Only cite quotations
C. Quote and cite source
D. Cite all the sources of the page

Fig. 9.8: How can shushma use information?

(**Source:** based on review of literature)

Ques. 3. Plagiarism does not consists of using which of the following without attributions

A. Ideas and images created by other
B. Modified Writing
C. Common knowledge
D. Your evaluated work

Fig. 9.9: Plagiarism does not consists of using

(**Source:** based on review of literature)

Ques. 4. John is particularly heart-breaking character, full of bluster as he tries to make sense of his abandonment by his abusive father and his well-meaning but immature mother. Which of the following are acceptable ways to use this text in your paper?

A. John is very heart-breaking character, full of emotion as he tries to understand his abandonment by his father (Hynes, 2006).
B. John's weakness is demonstrated by his obsession with the poor treatment from his father and mother (Hynes, 2006)
C. Either A and B
D. Neither A nor B

Fig. 9.10: John is particularly heart-braking character

(**Source:** based on review of literature)

Ques. 5. Sam wants to include an image of Van Gogh's "sunflowers" in his thesis. How can he do it?

A. A brief citation under the image

B. A full citation in the bibliography

C. Both A and B

D. It's old, so considered "Public Domain" and doesn't need to be cited.

Fig. 9.11: Sam wants to include an image of

(**Source:** based on review of literature)

Ques. 1. What is path writing?

A. Piecing together copied words from several papers into a paper of your own

B. Putting parenthetic citations in your paper. i.e. (Williams, 34)

C. Writing a paper with parenthetical citations, but no work cited page.

D. Writing a paper with parenthetical citations with work cited page

Fig. 9.12: What is patch writing?

(**Source:** based on review of literature)

Ques. 2. What is the best definition of paraphrasing?

A. Re-writing a statement into your own words

B. Taking a large amount of text and condensing it into a smaller amount

C. Changing one or two words in the text so that it is not exactly the same as the original

D. Using exact original words

Fig. 9.13: what is the best definition of paraphrasing?

(**Source:** based on review of literature)

Ques. 3. What is not a penalty if you are caught plagiarizing your work?

A. Could fail class or assignment
B. Could get expelled from university
C. Must pay fine to the college
D. Library privileges are revoked

Fig. 9.14: Penalty if you are caught plagiarizing your work?

(**Source:** based on review of literature)

Ques. 4. What is it that you don't do if you are unsure about rules dealing with plagiarism or citing your material?

A. Ask a librarian
B. Make an educated guess
C. Ask your professor
D. Ask a writing tutor

Fig. 9.15: Unsure about rules dealing with plagiarism or citing your materials?

(**Source:** based on review of literature)

Ques. 5. What are the consequences of plagiarism?

A. Tarnished reputation
B. Loss of job
C. Self Guilt
D. Monetary loss

Fig. 9.16: Consequences of plagiarism

(**Source:** based on review of literature)

1. Who is responsible for plagiarism? Students, teachers, or the institutions?
2. Why the problem of Plagiarism is more serious in India than in European Countries?

3. Why even after multiple policies, plagiarism still prevails in student assignments if not in thesis or dissertations?
4. Why do we, in India, need to focus more on teaching plagiarism extensively in classrooms? Please give ample examples to justify your answers. Your examples can be from any scenario - social, political, economic, society and so on.
5. How bad is plagiarism? Should we take it seriously in even classroom based non-evaluated tasks or evaluated assignments? Or should we just take it seriously at research level?

Food for thought!!!

- Have you ever given zero to a student in an assignment because the student copied the assignment? If no, why not?
- Have you ever felt that students' act of copying assignment was justified and passed the student. If yes, what were the justifications?
- Have you ever copied someone else's words and didn't acknowledge them?

Now…

- Imagine someone presenting your words, ideas and work and getting credit of years' of your hard work.

TASK (Group Activity)

- As teachers, we need to teach plagiarism
- How do you teach plagiarism?
- Design some activities to teach a particular aspect of plagiarism.

REFERENCES

First Photo. Http://www.Plagiarismchecker.Net/plagiarism-pictures.Php accessed on 07/04/2017

Second Photo. Tes Teach Website. https://www.tes.com/lessons/fGE8wZ1YtRtaCQ/plagiarism last accessed on 07/04/2017

Adapted from Plagiarism Game. The Lycoming College website, Williamsport. http://www.lycoming.edu/library/instruction/tutorials/plagiarismGame.aspx last accessed on 07/04/2017

Scientific Writing and Research Quality
Edited by: Dr. Prasann Kumar & Dr. Pawan Kumar 'Bharti'
ISBN: 978-93-88854-48-1
Edition: 2020
Published by: Discovery Publishing House Pvt. Ltd., New Delhi (India)

Pages 87-96

10 Research Towards Research Excellence in Research

Prasann Kumar[1,2]* & Shipa Rani Dey[1]

GRAPHICAL ABSTRACT

Keywords: Academic, Biology, Excellence, Research, Science

Introduction

- A research articleis not complete until it has been read and interpreted; it is a process that includes the readers. Ex. A film must be seen and interpreted and includes its audience.
- The scientific document must be written well. Ex. The credit for a discovery goes to a person who first convinces the world, not necessarily to the person who first makes the discovery.
- IDEA-DO RESEARCH-WRITE PAPERS.
- The difficulty faced (by many) in reading a large fraction of the scientific literature is not due to the complexity of scientific concepts, but is due to these difficult-to-read documents being poorly written.

[1] Department of Agronomy, School of Agriculture, Lovely Professional University, Jalandhar, Punjab, India, 144411

[2] Divison of Research and Development, Lovely Professional University, Jalandhar, Punjab, India, 144411

- A research paper reports new data or hypothesis.
- It goes through the peer process of reviewing before printing.

Pre-requisites of Writing Research Paper

1. Structural Principles
2. Order and Organization
3. A Matter of Style

1. Structural Principles: The purpose of a research paper is to communicate, not merely present, data or ideas.

Reader Expectations

- A paper can be read at several levels:
  - Some people just will refer to the title
  - Others may read only the title and abstract
  - Others will read the paperfor a deeper understanding
- Readers do not read: they interpret.
- Reader's expectation is to link the substance of pros based on cluesthey receive from its structure.
- Since we read from left to right, we prefer the context, the familiar element, on the left, and the new, intriguing information on the right.
- Avoid plagiarism.

Unit of Discourse

Each unit of discourse, a sentence, a paragraph or a section should serve a single function, to make a single point.

The Subject and its Verb

- Consider the following sentence

  "The greatest Italian navigator, who was funded by queen Isabella of Spain to sail west from Europe to discover a new route to the east but ended up on the American continent in the late fifteenth century to set in motion a great wave of migration from Europe, was Christopher Columbus."
- The problem (lies with the structural position of the clause):
- **De-phrasing the sentence, even without splitting into two, helps the reader.**

  "The greatest Italian navigator was Christopher Columbus; he was funded by queen Isabella of Spain to sail west from Europe to discover a new route to the east, but ended up on the American continent in the late fifteenth century to set in motion a great wave of migration from Europe."

The Stress Position

- The end of the sentence is called the stress position. It is here that the eaders naturally expect to find the**emphatic part.**
- Consider the following two sentences and find the stress position.
  - (*i*) The Circuit training method was developed by **R.E. Morgan and G.T. Anderson.**
  - (*ii*) Strength endurance can be best developed through**circuit training method.**
- The size of the stress position is not fixed: it may be a single word, or may extend to several lines.
- Within a sentence, secondary stress positions can be created by using colons or semi-colons, e.g. in 1.3 above.
- Thus, it is not length of the sentence that matters, but the effective use of the stress positions to create and transfer emphasis.

The Topic Position

- The beginning position is called the topic position, which links backward to the previous discussion and provides the context of new information to follow.
- **Example: In our example in 1.4, the first sentence tells us about the research of R.E. Morgan and G.T. Anderson, and the second about the Circuit training method.**
- When the **new information** is important enough to receive emphasis, it functions best **in the stress position.**
- Put in the **topic position** the **old information t**hat links backward; put in the stress position the new information you want the reader to emphasis.
- **Example: 'Topic position' is exploited in the television serials when a new episode is started with a recap of the previous episode, providing backward connection.**

2. Organization and Order: Research paper follows some order: (*i*) Abstract; (*ii*) introduction; (*iii*) Materials and Methods; (*iv*) Results; (*v*) Discussion; (*vi*) References

Abstract

Usually restricted to 250 words, and includes discussion on

(*i*) **Why:** The objective of the investigation.

(*ii*) **How:** The methodology in brief.

(*iii*) **What:** The results of the investigation in brief.

(*iv*) **Keywords**

Avoid: (*i*) Information that is not contained in the paper; (*ii*) References.

Body of the Research Paper

Introduction and objectives

- Provide rationale for the investigation (Articulating the issue).
- Provide relevant background for the investigation: sensitizing the readers with the context and the justification.
- While reviewing the background literature, avoid listing references serially: X did this; Y did this; and Z did that.
- Provide a coherent summary of earlier work, grouping these as required.
- Last paragraph presents concisely the issue proposed to be investigated.

Materials and methods

- Technical description of material and method should be precise but detailed enough to enable a person to follow the experiment/test and repeat them.
- If the method is new, ***all*** details must be provided.
- If the method has been previously published in a scientific journal, only the reference should be given with some identification.
- Organize the methods under subheadings, with related methods described together (e.g. subjects, experimental design, Measurement of…, etc…).

Results

- Begin the section with a brief statement of the rationale or objective and an overview of the methods used.
- Then present the results of investigation.
- Do not repeat in the text what is obvious in the tables and figures.
- Redundancy should be avoided.

Discussion

- Long-winded and meandering discussion, or claims not supported by the results should be avoided.
- Discuss results, relationships among the variables that can be inferred and the generalizations that can be deduced from the results.
- Avoid repetitions.
- Make comparisons, if possible, with other published works, and show similarities and contrast with them.

References

The research papers quoted should be included in the list of references, the format of which, like the format of citation in the text, depends on the journal.

(*a*) **Harvard Reference Style:** Zope, AS &Zope, AR 2013, 'Sudarshankriya yoga: Breathing for health' Int J Yoga, Vol. 6, No.1, pp. 4–10.

(*b*) **Vancouver Reference Style:** Zope AS, Zope, AR. Sudarshankriya yoga: Breathing for health. Int J Yoga. 2013; 6(1): 4–10.

(*c*) **APA Reference Style:** Zope, A.S., &Zope, A.R. (2013). Sudarshankriya yoga: Breathing for health. *Int J Yoga.* 6(1), 4–10.

A Matter of Style

- Follow basic rule of grammar and usage.

Clarity

- Scientific terminology carries precise meaning and must be used with care.
- Avoid using a cesspool of language.
- Put statements in positive form.

Example: Prefer 'dishonest' to 'not honest'

Example: 'Rained everyday' better than 'unfavorable weather'.

Brevity

- Be concise; omit needless words.
- A paragraph should not contain any unnecessary words, for the same reason that a drawing should have no unnecessary lines and a machine no unnecessary parts.
- Use active voice; minimize use of passive words.

Tense: Use

- Present tense to state a previously published results that is accepted as fact.
- Put past tense to report your results (because not yet accepted once;
- Pat perfect tense (had been) to indicate the action hat happened before other past actions;
- Present perfect (have) to indicate an action recently completed or continuing to the present;
- Present tense to refer to other parts of the paper.

Tables and Figures

- Whether to present the data in text, tables, or in figures depends on the volume of the data and on whether ratio a trend.

- When tabulating data, ensure
  (*i*) material reads down not across;
  (*ii*) Tables must carry a caption, and the units in which data are expressed;
- Additional material should be put in explanatory forms (not too be mixed up in caption).
- Do not clutter a graph with more lines then can be interpreted with ease.

Steps to Writing Better (Four Steps to Follow)

- **First:** Plan the paper. Organize thoughts and prepare an outline.
- **Second:** Write the first draft using the outline.
  - Avoid interruptions in the process of thought;
  - Do not revise while writing, else it break thought process and its flow.
- **Third:** Keep the draft aside and allow some time to become capable of taking an objective view of the draft.
- **Fourth**: Revision: Revise the draft. In revising, go over the draft five times.

(*i*) Concentrate on paper contents on following lines:
  (*a*) Does the paper contain all that my readers need?
  (*b*) How much material can be removed without interfering with the reader's understanding needs.

(*ii*) Strive for clarity; correct positioning of word in a sentence and correct use of punctuation is critical.

(*iii*) **Correct grammar:** One may have to go for several rounds of rewriting.

(*iv*) **Brevity:** eliminate all un necessary words. Avoid repetitions.

(*v*) **Improve the style:** Ensure that
  (*a*) Sections connect well to form the paper;
  (*b*) Paragraph connect well to form the sections;
  (*c*) Sentences connect well to form paragraphs.

Fig. 10.1: Plagiarism

(**Source:** based on review of literature)

All of the Following are Considered Plagiarism

- turning in someone else's work as your own
- copying words or ideas from someone else without giving credit
- failing to put a quotation in quotation marks
- giving incorrect information about the source of a quotation
- changing words but copying the sentence structure of a source without giving credit copying so many words or ideas from a source that it makes up the majority of your work, whether you give credit or not

Plagiarism v. Paraphrasing Samples

- **Direct quote from research:** "Japan's beautiful Mount Fuji last erupted in 1707 and is now classified as dormant. Dormant volcanoes show no signs of activity, but they may erupt in the future."
- **Non-plagiarized paraphrase:** Mount Fuji, the highest mountain in Japan, is actually a dormant volcano. Dormant means that it is not active. The last time Mount Fuji erupted was in 1707, and there is always the possibility of a future eruption.

Selection of Journal?

- Deciding the journal to which the manuscript is to be sent and going through its Guidelines for authors for preparing manuscripts

Author Priorities for Journal Selection

- Key (Determining) factors
  - Impact Factor
  - Reputation
  - Access to the target audience
  - Overall editorial standard
  - Publication speed
  - International coverage
  - Open Access

Source of Selection?

- Go for journals website

Source of Selection?

- Go for journals website
  www.indianjournals.com
  www.springer.com
  www.medknow.com
  www.ias.ac.in
  www.tandf.co.uk

Fig. 10.2: Source of selection?

(**Source:** based on review of literature)

Journal Impact Factor

- A measure of the frequency with which the average article in a **journal** has been cited in a particular year.
- **Calculation of an impact factor** is based upon the average number of citations received per paper published in a particular journal during the preceding two years.
- 2015 Impact Factor = α / β.
- α = the number of times that articles published by a particular journal in 2013 and 2014 were cited by other indexed journals in 2013 and 2014.
- β = the total number of articles and other submitted works published by that journal in 2013 and 2014.

EX: 200 Citation in 2013 and 2014, and 50 articles published in two years.

- Then impact factor = 200/50 = 4.
- **h-index.**
- In 2005, physicist Jorge E. Hirsch developed the h-index as a process for *quantifying the output of an individual researcher.*
- *h-index is the largest number h such that h publications have at least h citations.*
- Web of Science, Scopus, and Google Scholar can also be used to calculate an h-index for that particular citation-tracking database.
- To calculate your h-index, organize articles in descending order, based on the number of times they have been cited *(see below example).*
- In the below example, an author has 7 papers. This tells us that the author's h-index is 6.

Articles Citation Numbers

1 33

2 30

3 20

4 15

5 7

<u>6 6</u>

7 5

- An h-index of 6 means that this author has published at least 6 papers that have each received at least 6 citations.

i-10-Index

Fig. 10.3: i-10-index

(**Source:** based on review of literature)

Article Submission

- Select your journal carefully
- Read the aims and scope
- Think about your target audience and the level of your work – do you have a realistic chance of being accepted?
- **Follow the guidelines** in the notes for authors and include everything they ask – it makes the editor's job easier…
- Articles should **not** be submitted to more than one journal at a time
- Most journal editors will make an initial decision on a paper - to review or to reject
- Most editors appoint two referees
- Refereeing speed varies tremendously between journals

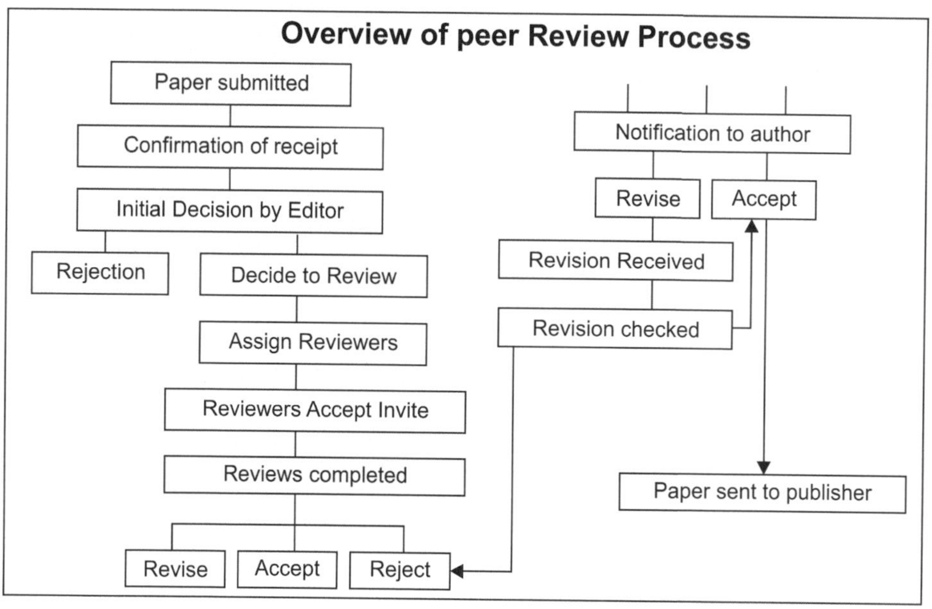

Figu. 10.4: Overview of Peer Review Process

(**Source:** based on review of literature)

- Authors should receive a decision of Accept, Accept with Revision (Minor or Major), or Reject
- If a paper is rejected, most editors will write to you explaining their decision
- After rejection, authors have the option of submitting the paper to another journal - editor's suggestions should be addressed

REFERENCES

https://www.aresearchguide.com/1steps.html

https://writing.wisc.edu/Handbook/PlanResearchPaper.html

https://writing.wisc.edu/handbook/assignments/planresearchpaper/

https://owl.purdue.edu/owl/general_writing/...writing.../research_papers/index.html

Scientific Writing and Research Quality
Edited by: Dr. Prasann Kumar & Dr. Pawan Kumar 'Bharti'
ISBN: 978-93-88854-48-1
Edition: 2020
Published by: Discovery Publishing House Pvt. Ltd., New Delhi (India)

Pages 97-108

11

Microarrys
Insight for Research

Prasann Kumar[1,2]* & Shipa Rani Dey[1]

GRAPHICAL ABSTRACT

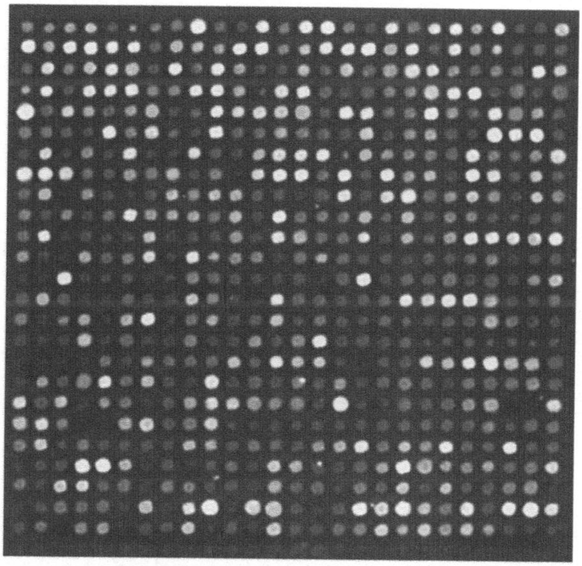

Keywords: *Biology, Crop, DNA, Micro, RNA*

Introduction

- The central dogma of life forms
- DNA
- RNA
- Monitoring the expression of genes

[1] Department of Agronomy, School of Agriculture, Lovely Professional University, Jalandhar, Punjab, India, 144411

[2] Divison of Research and Development, Lovely Professional University, Jalandhar, Punjab, India, 144411

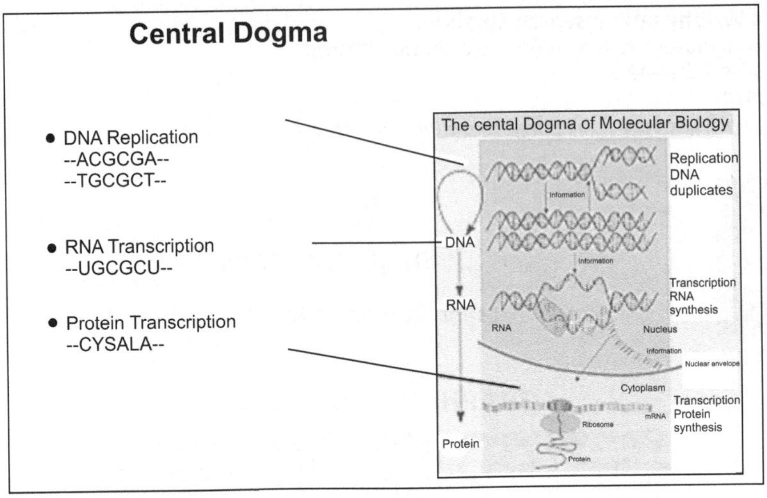

Fig. 11.1: Central Dogma

(**Source:** based on review of literature)

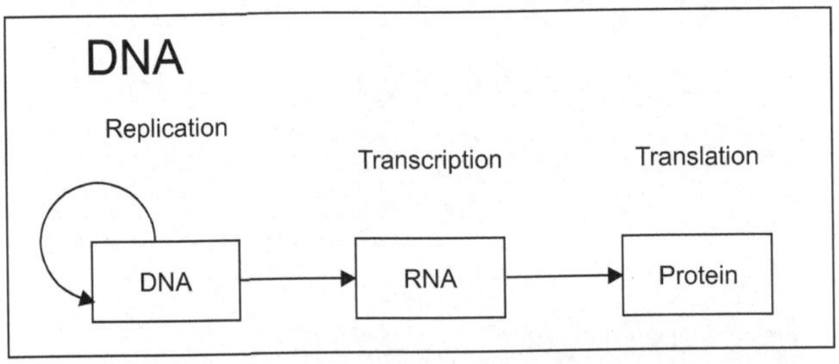

Fig. 11.2: Information flow

(**Source:** based on review of literature)

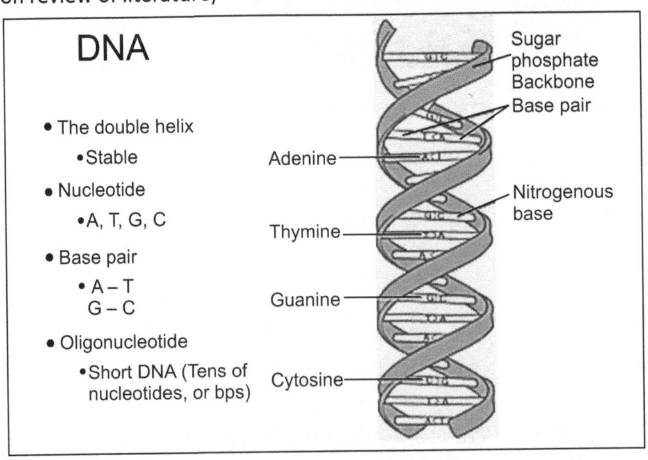

Fig. 11.3: DNA and its structure

(**Source:** based on review of literature)

DNA Strand

DNA has cononical orientation

Read from 5' to 3'

Antiparallel: one strand has direction to its complement's

5' ......TACTGAA ......3'
3' ......ATGACTT ...... 5'

Fig. 11.4: DNA strand

(**Source:** based on review of literature)

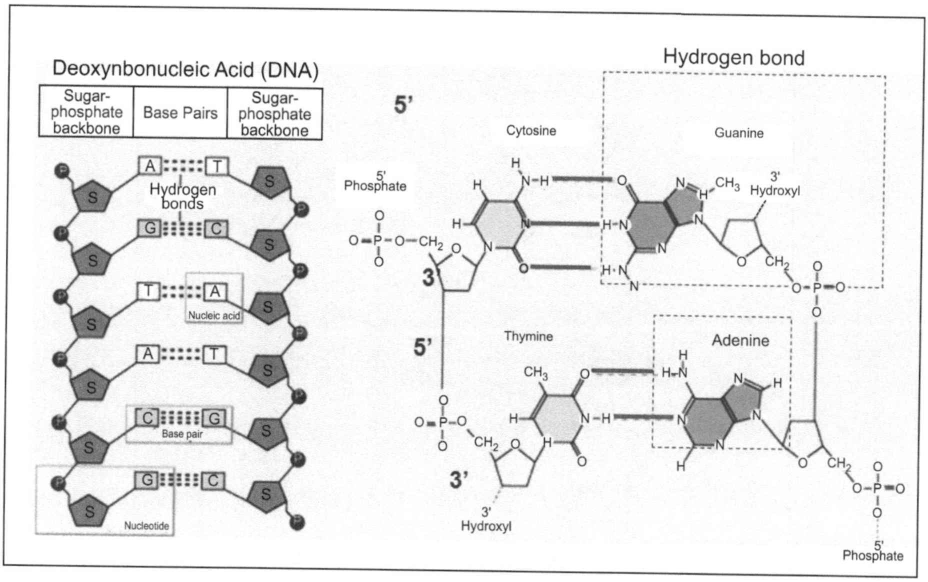

Fig. 11.5: Hydrogen bond

(**Source:** based on review of literature)

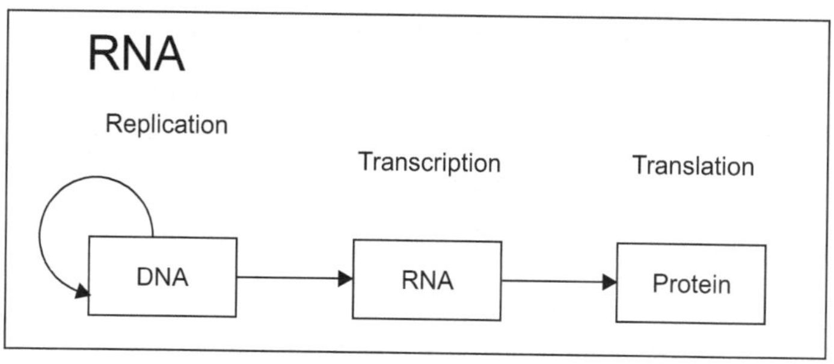

Fig. 11.6: RNA and its information

(**Source:** based on review of literature)

RNA

- Types
  - messenger RNA
  - ribosomal RNA (rRNA)
  - transfer RNA (tRNA)

Gene is expressed by transcribing DNA into single-stranded mRNA

Fig. 11.7: RNA and its type

(**Source:** based on review of literature)

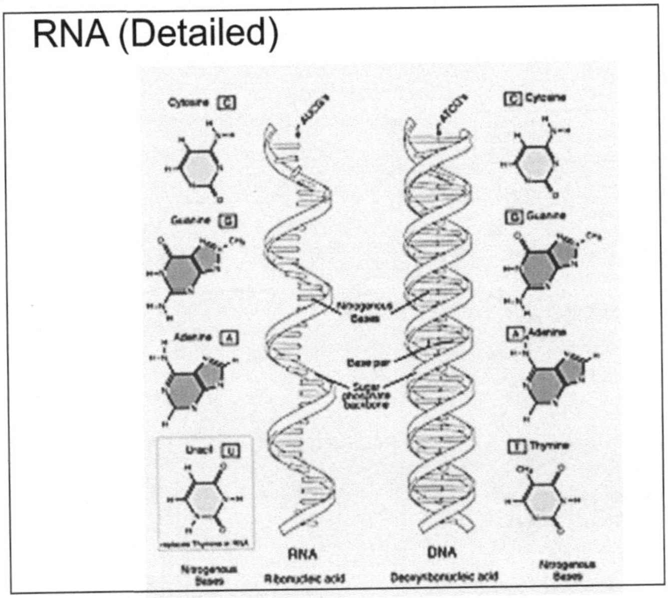

Fig. 11.8: RNA detailed

(**Source:** based on review of literature)

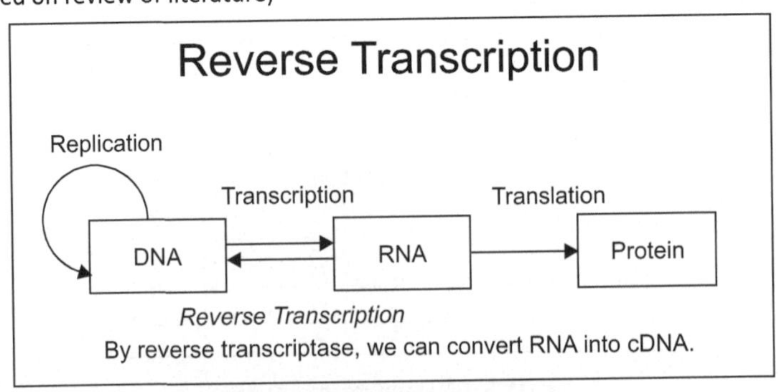

Fig. 11.9: Reverse Transcription

(**Source:** based on review of literature)

The Southern Blot

- Basic DNA detection technique that has been used for over 30 years, known as Southern blots:
  - A "known" strand of DNA is deposited on a solid support (i.e. nitocellulose paper).
  - An "unknown" mixed bag of DNA is labelled (radioactive or flourescent).
  - "Unknown" DNA solution allowed to mix with known DNA (attached to nitro paper), then excess solution washed off.
  - If a copy of "known" DNA occurs in "unknown" sample, it will stick (hybridize), and labeled DNA will be detected on photographic film.

mRNA Represent Gene Function

- When measure the level of the mRNA, we are monitoring the activity of a gene.
- Thus, if we can understand all the level of mRNAs, we can study the expression of whole genome.
- Microarray takes the advantage of getting over 10000 of blotting data in a single experiment, which makes monitoring the genome activity possible.

What are Microarrays?

- Microarrays are simply small glass or silicon slides upon the surface of which are arrayed thousands of genes (usually between 500 up to a million).
- Using a conventional *hybridization* process, the level of expression of genes is measured (for instance).
- Microarrays are read using laser-based fluorescence scanners.
- The process is "high throughput".

Why use Microarrays?

- Determine what genes are active in a cell and at what levels.
- Compare the gene expression profiles of a control vs treated.
- Determine what genes have increased or decreased in during an experimental condition.
- Determine which genes have biological significance in a system.
- Discovery of new genes, pathways, and cellular trafficking.

Why analyze so many genes?

- Just because we sequenced a genome doesn't mean we know anything about the genes. Thousands of genes remain without an assigned function.

- Patterns or clusters of genes are more informative regarding total cellular function than looking at one or two genes – can figure out new pathways

mRNA Levels Compared in Many Different Contexts

- Different tissues, same organism (brain v. liver)
- Same tissue, same organism (tumor v. non-tumor)
- Same tissue, different organisms (wt v. mutant)
- Time course experiments (development)
- Other special designs (e.g. to detect spatial patterns).

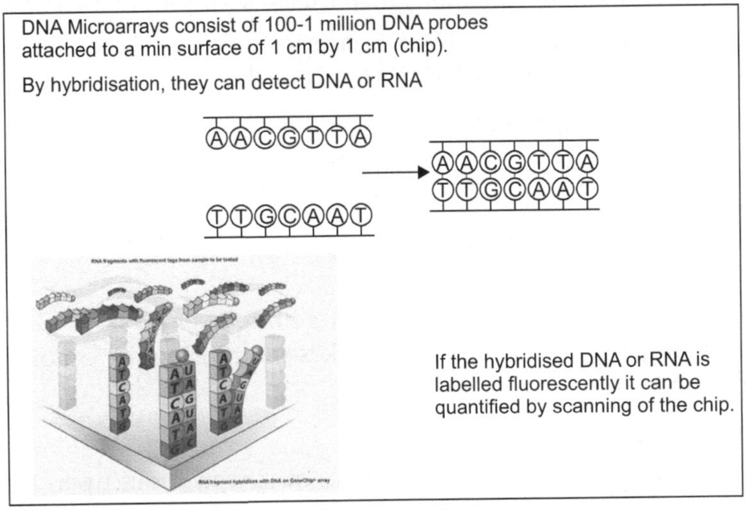

Fig. 11.10: DNA Microarrays

(**Source:** based on review of literature)

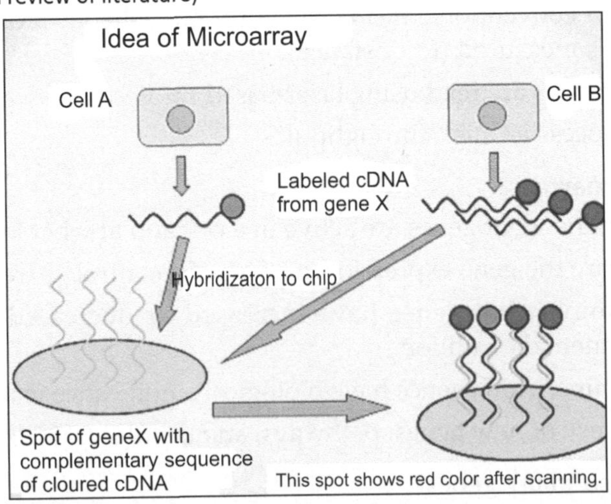

Fig. 11.11: Idea of microarray

(**Source:** based on review of literature)

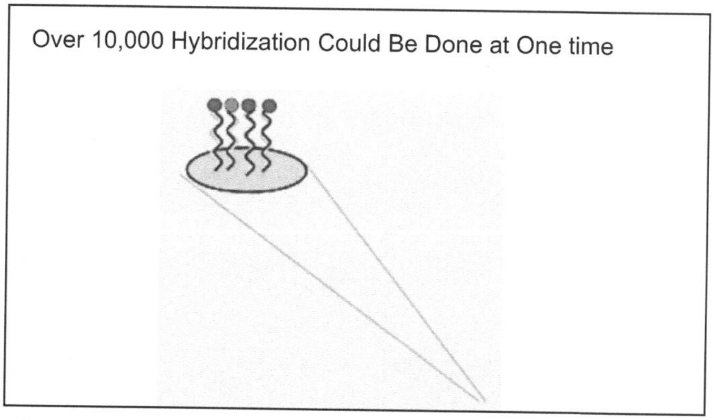

Fig. 11.12: Hybridization

(**Source:** based on review of literature)

DNA Microarrays can be Manufactured by

- Inkjet (Agilent, Canon)
- Robot spotting (many providers)

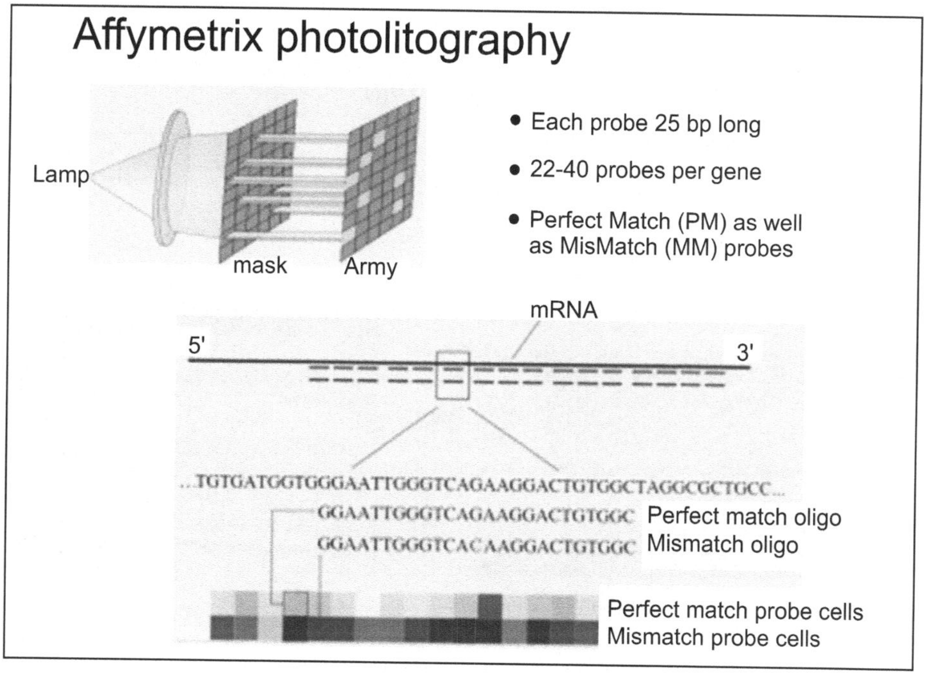

Fig. 11.13: Affymetrix photolithography

(**Source:** based on review of literature)

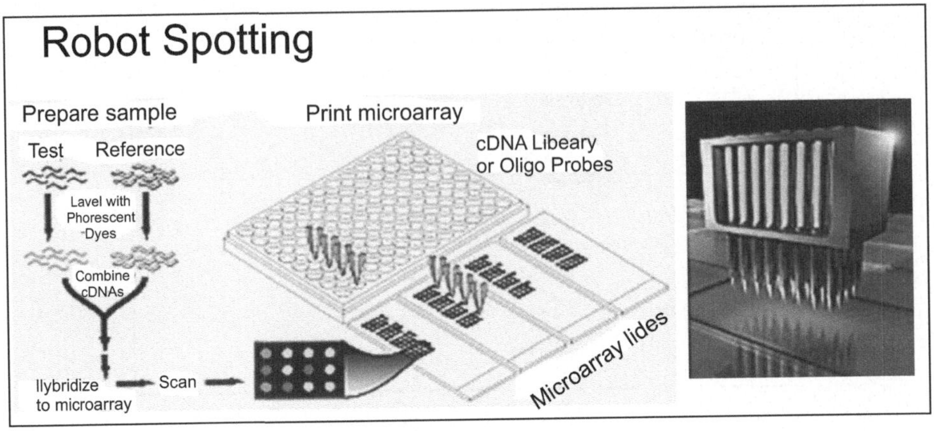

Fig. 11.14: Robot spotting

(**Source:** based on review of literature)

Array Fabrication Spotting

- Use PCR to amplify DNA
- Robotic "pen" deposits DNA at defined coordinates
- approximately 1-10 ng per spot
- Experimentation with oligos (40, 70 bp)

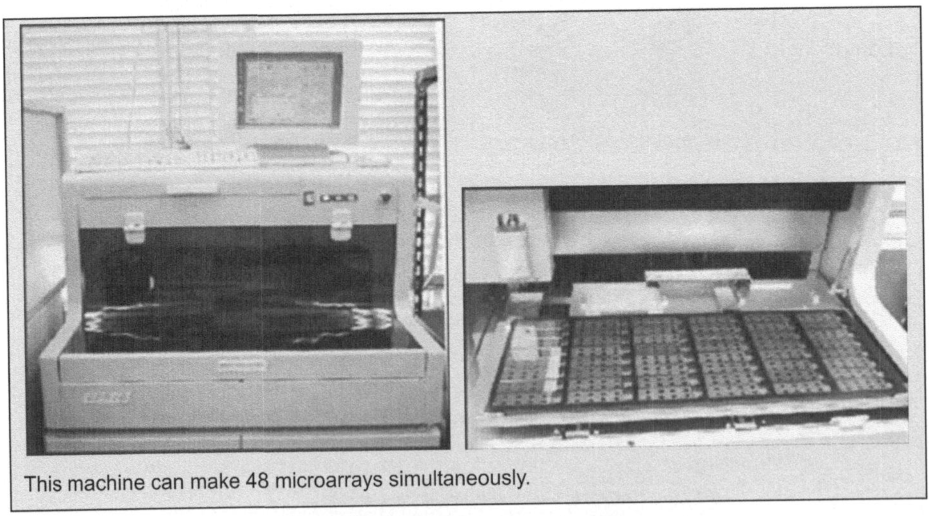

Fig. 11.15: Machine for microarray

(**Source:** based on review of literature)

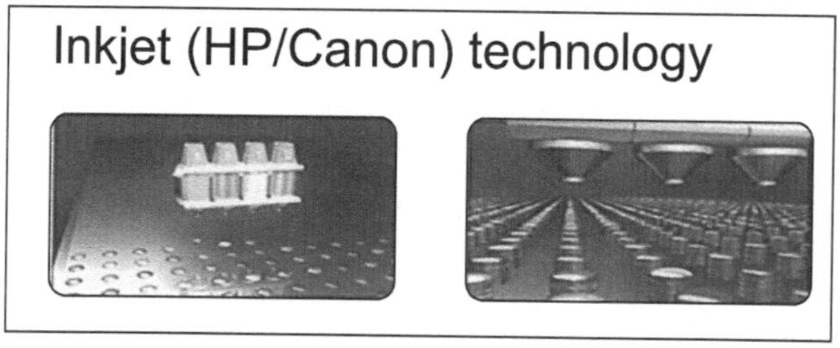

Fig. 11.16: Inkjet (HP/Canon) technology

(**Source:** based on review of literature)

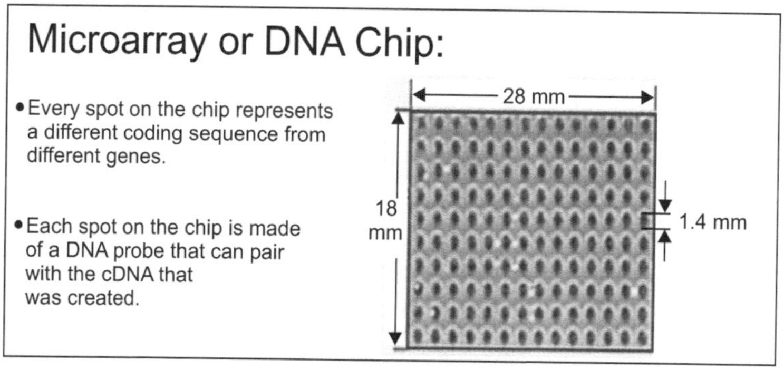

Fig. 11.17: Microarray or DNA Chip

(**Source:** based on review of literature)

Types of Microarray

- Pre-synthesized nucleic acids.
- Bought cDNA.
- Oligonucleotide synthesis *in situ*.
- Creating cDNA in question.

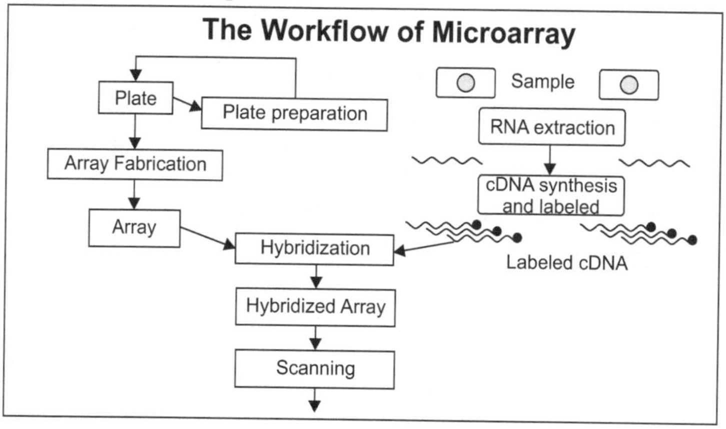

Fig. 11.18: Workflow of microarray

(**Source:** based on review of literature)

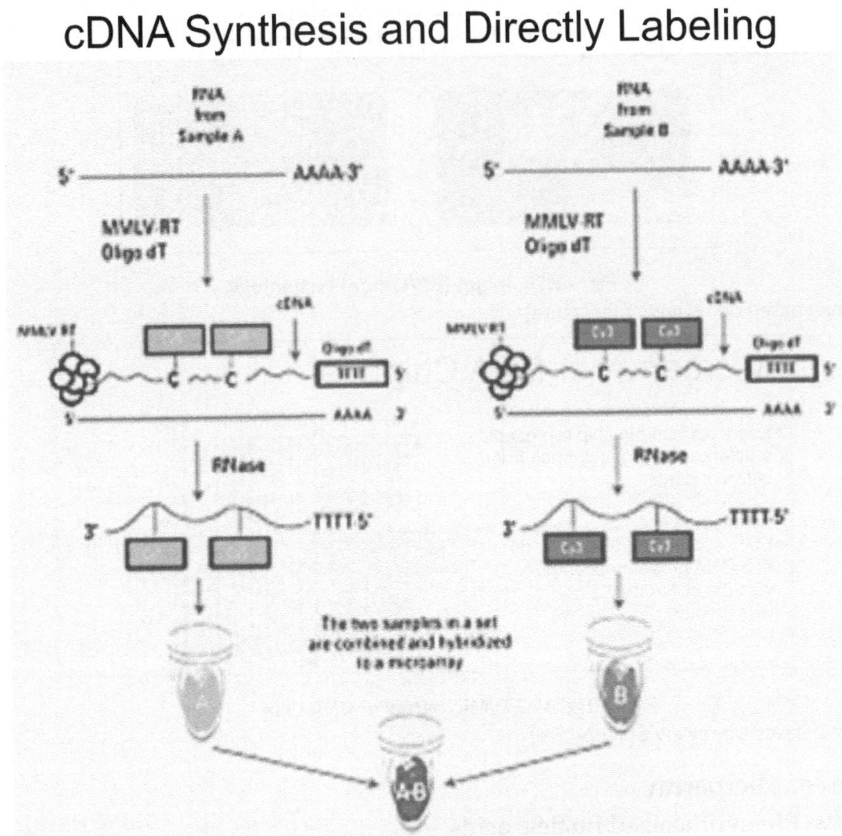

Fig. 11.19: cDNA synthesis and Directly Labeling

(**Source:** based on review of literature)

Basic Steps to Microarray

- Obtain cells with genes that are needed for analysis.
- Isolate the mRNA using extraction buffer.
- Remove the buffer with RNA.
- The mRNA will be 5′-3′ with repeating AAA..end.
- Convert each mRNA into colored cDNA.
- Targets labeled with fluorophores.
- With mRNA degraded reverse cDNA created.
- Mix colored samples of cDNA.
- Incubation with the mixed cDNA and the chip DNA will yield some pairing.
- Wash off unbound cDNA to see what has bound to the microarray.

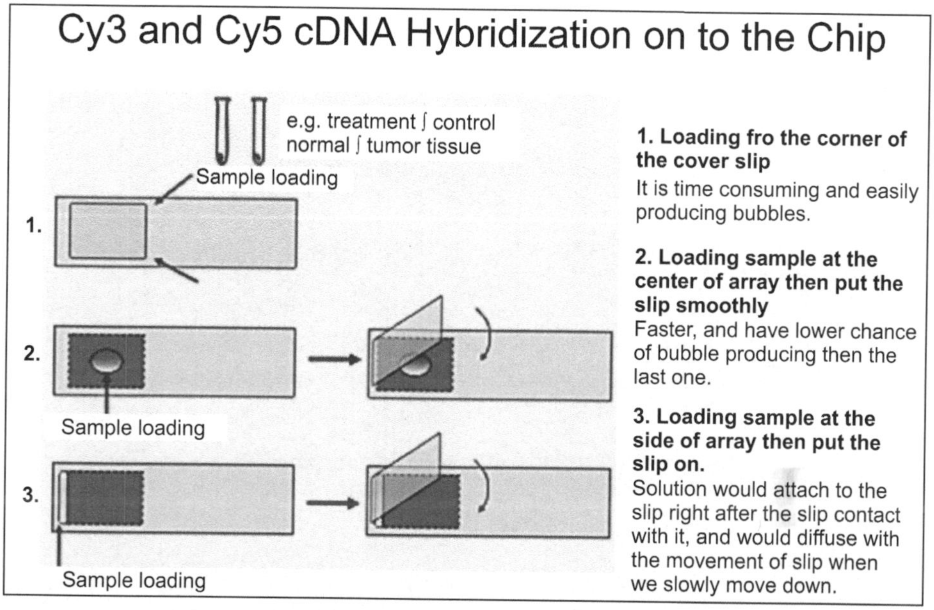

Fig. 11.20: Cy3 and Cy5 cDNA Hybridization

(**Source:** based on review of literature)

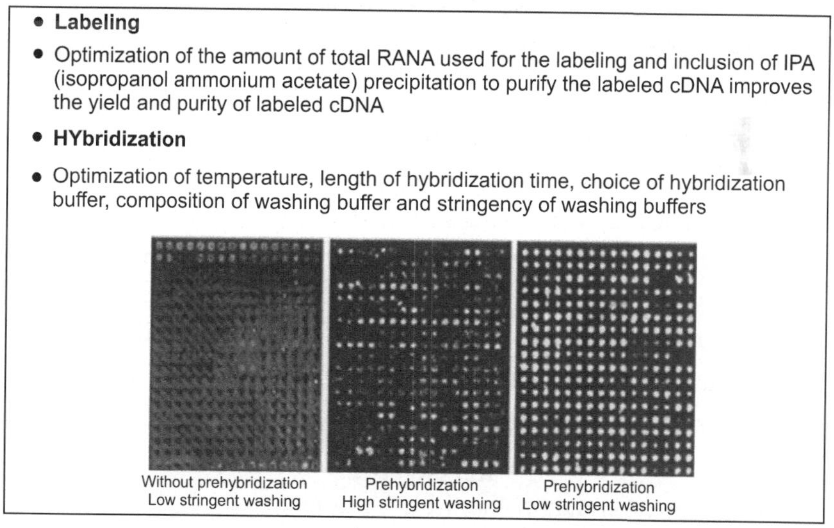

Fig. 11.21: Labeling and Hybridization

(**Source:** based on review of literature)

Visualizing Bound cDNA

- The slide with the microarray chip is placed inside a dark box where it is scanned with a high resolution laser that detects the bound fluorescent labels.

- The information and images are then sent to the computer for analysis.

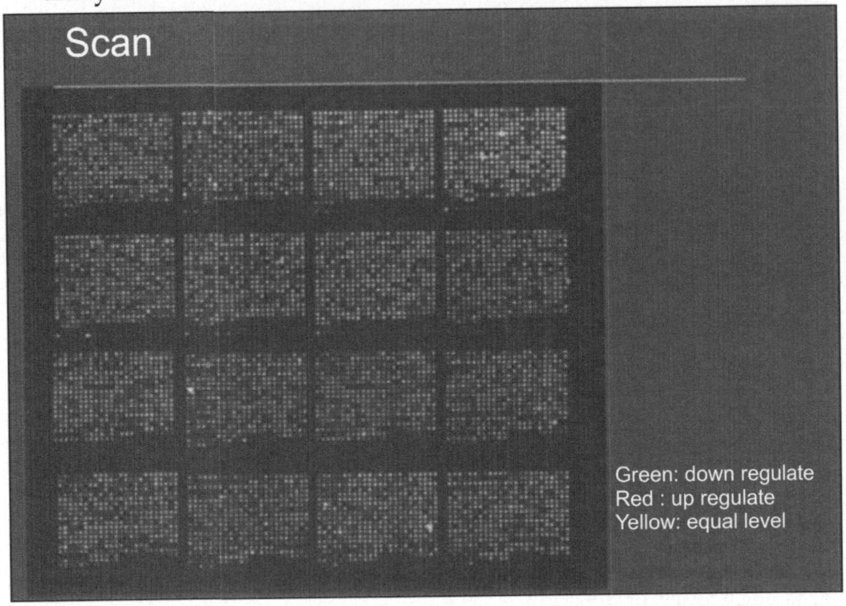

Fig. 11.22: Scan results

(**Source:** based on review of literature)

Conclusion

- Technology is evolving rapidly
- Blending of biology, automation, and informatics
- New applications are being pursued
- Beyond gene discovery into screening, validation, clinical genotyping, etc.
- Microarrays are becoming more broadly available and accepted
- Protein Arrays, tissue arrays, etc.
- Diagnostic Applications

REFERENCES

Genomics, gene expression and DNA arrays (Nature, June 2000)

http://www.lsic.ucla.edu/ls3/tutorials/

Microarray - technology review (Natural Cell Biology, Aug. 2001)

Magic of Microarray (Scientific American, Feb. 2002)

Molecular biology tutorial

Review papers on microarray

Scientific Writing and Research Quality
Edited by: Dr. Prasann Kumar & Dr. Pawan Kumar 'Bharti'
ISBN: 978-93-88854-48-1
Edition: 2020
Published by: Discovery Publishing House Pvt. Ltd., New Delhi (India)
Pages 109-118

12 Research Progress and Its Understanding

Prasann Kumar[1,2*]

GRAPHICAL ABSTRACT

Keywords: Agriculture, Crop, Development, Research, Progress

Introduction

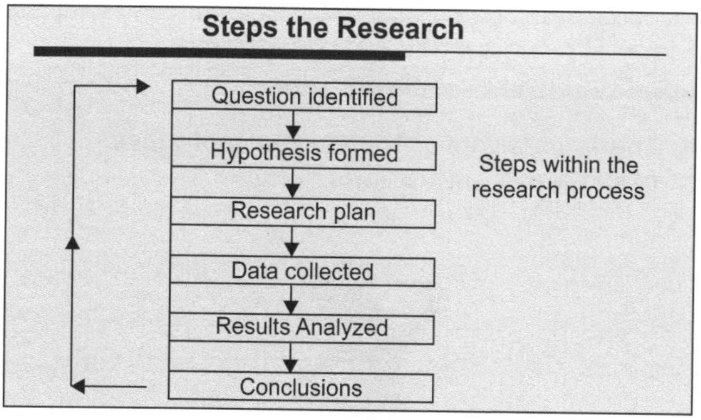

Fig. 12.1: Basic of Research Stages
(**Source:** based on review of literature)

[1] Department of Agronomy, School of Agriculture, Lovely Professional University, Jalandhar, Punjab, India, 144411
[2] Divison of Research and Development, Lovely Professional University, Jalandhar, Punjab, India, 144411

Steps in Conducting Research

- Specific steps guide the research process
- Number of steps is indeterminate
- Various steps may be combined
- Order of steps may vary somewhat
- Importance of specific steps is variable
- "12 Steps of Research"

"12 Steps of Research"

1. Identify the research question
2. Initial review of literature
3. Distilling the question to a researchable problem
4. Continued review of literature
5. Formulation of hypothesis
6. Determining the basic research approach
7. Identifying the population and sample
8. Designing the data collection plan
9. Selecting or developing data collection instruments
10. Choosing the method of data analysis
11. Implementing the research plan
12. Interpreting the results

Fig. 12.2: 12 steps of Research

(**Source:** based on review of literature)

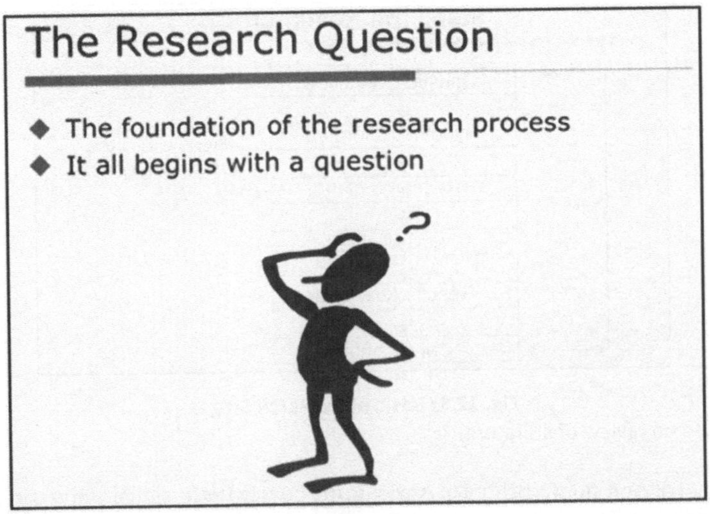

Fig. 12.3: Research question

(**Source:** based on review of literature)

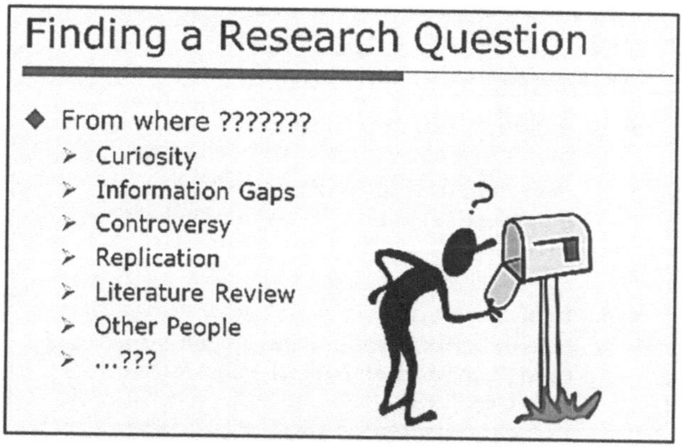

Fig. 12.4: Research question finding

(**Source:** based on review of literature)

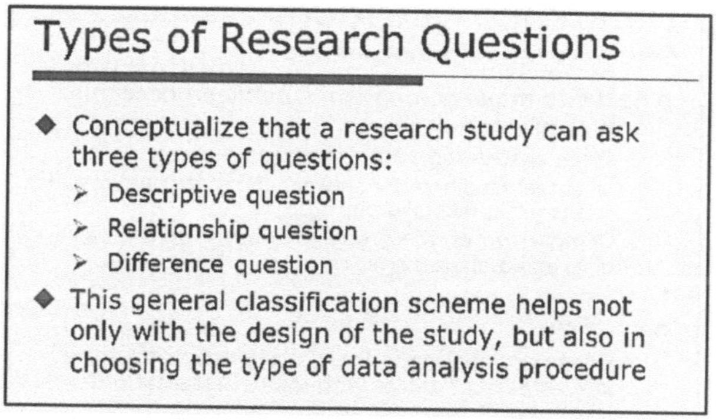

Fig. 12.5: Types of research questions

(**Source:** based on review of literature)

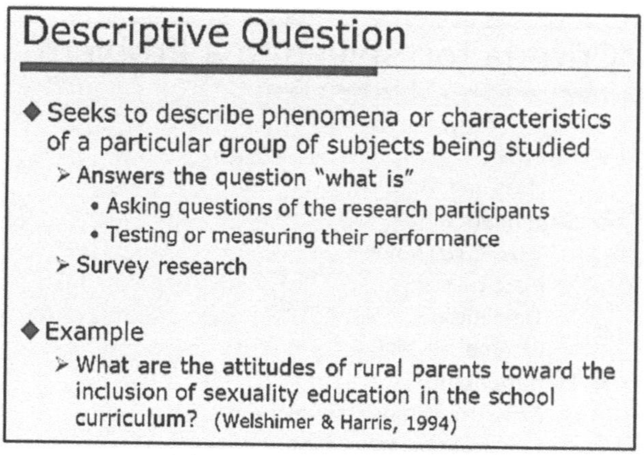

Fig. 12.6: Descriptive question

(**Source:** based on review of literature)

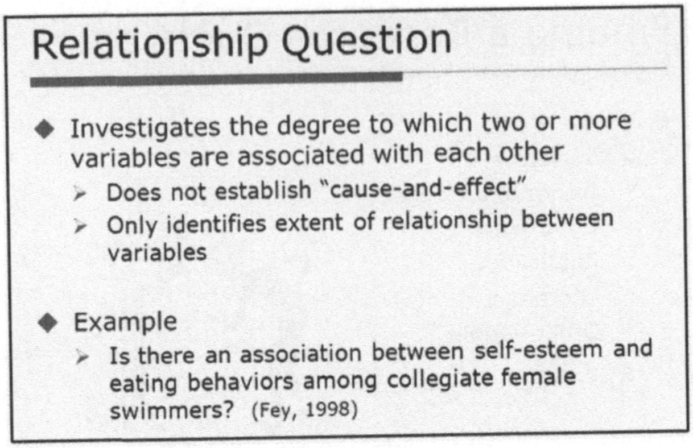

Fig. 12.7: Relationship question

(**Source:** based on review of literature)

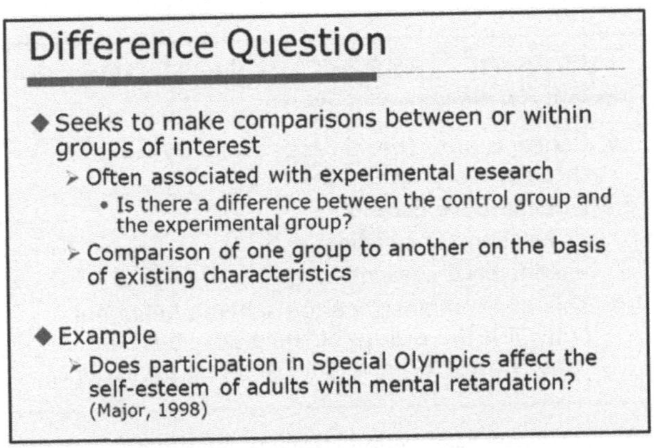

Fig. 12.8: Difference question

(**Source:** based on review of literature)

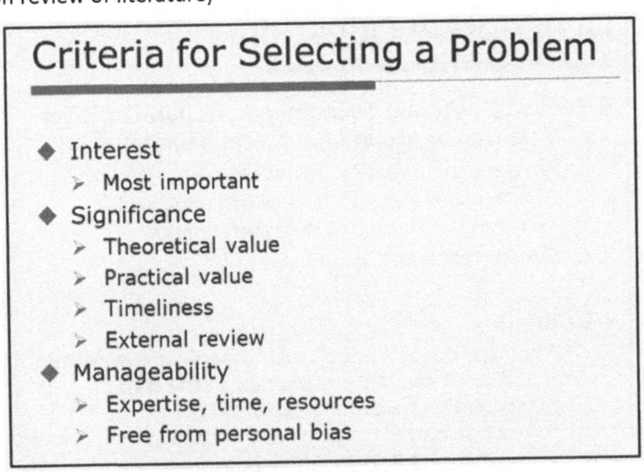

Fig. 12.9: Criteria for selecting a problem

(**Source:** based on review of literature)

Problem Distillation

- The process of refining the question or idea into a problem and making it sufficiently specific so that it is amenable to investigation
- This process should lead to the development of a "statement of the problem" that is clear, concise, and definitive

Fig. 12.10: Problem Distillation

(**Source:** based on review of literature)

Statement of the Problem

- A very specific statement which clearly identifies the problem being studied; will usually identify the key variables as well as give some information about the scope of the study
- May be in either question or declarative form
- May include inherent sub-problems, if appropriate
- Formulation of problem statement takes place after an initial review of related literature and the distillation process

Fig. 12.11: Statement of the problem

(**Source:** based on review of literature)

Problem Statements

- "The problem of this study was to ..."
- "This study was concerned with ..."
- "This study is designed to ..."
- "The purpose of this investigation is to ..."

Fig. 12.12: Problem statements

(**Source:** based on review of literature)

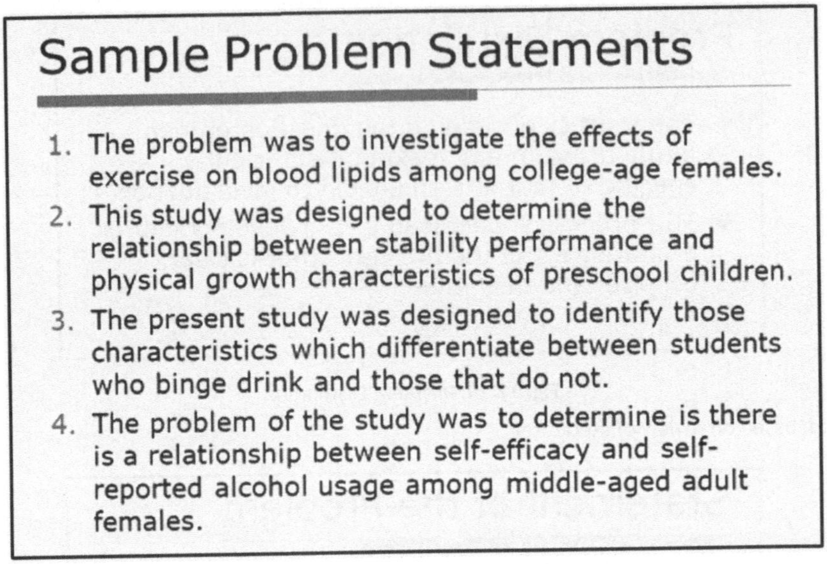

Fig. 12.13: Sample problem statements

(**Source:** based on review of literature)

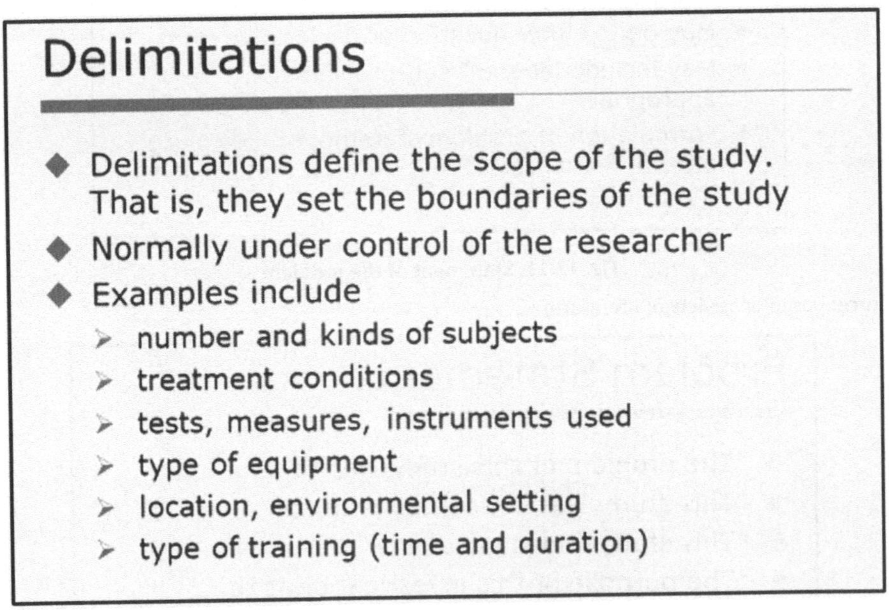

Fig. 12.14: Delimitations

(**Source:** based on review of literature)

Limitations

- Limitations are very similar to delimitations, but they tend to focus on potential weaknesses of the study
- Examples include
  - sampling problems (representativeness of subjects)
  - uncontrolled factors and extraneous variables
  - faulty research design and techniques
  - reliability and validity of measuring instruments
  - compromises to internal/external validity

Fig. 12.15: Limitations

(**Source:** based on review of literature)

Limitations continued

- Possible shortcomings of the study . . . usually cannot be controlled by the researcher
  - the researcher will, of course, try to eliminate extremely serious weaknesses before the study is commenced
- May be a result of assumptions not being met
- No study is perfect; the researcher recognizes the weaknesses

Fig. 12.16: Continuation of figure 16

(**Source:** based on review of literature)

Assumptions

- Assumptions are basic, fundamental conditions that must exist in order for the research to proceed
- Basic premises required in the study... the researcher does everything possible to increase the credibility of the assumptions, but does not have absolute control
- Assumptions could be made about (1) the motivation of the subjects, (2) whether subjects responded truthfully, (3) the validity of the measuring instrument, and (4) whether subjects followed directions correctly

Fig. 12.17: Assumptions

(**Source:** based on review of literature)

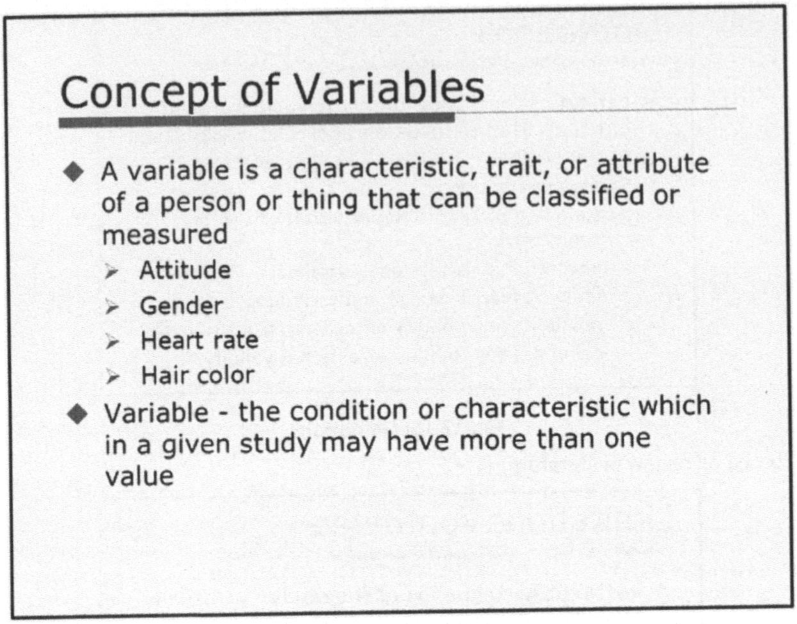

Fig. 12.18: Concept of Variables

(**Source:** based on review of literature)

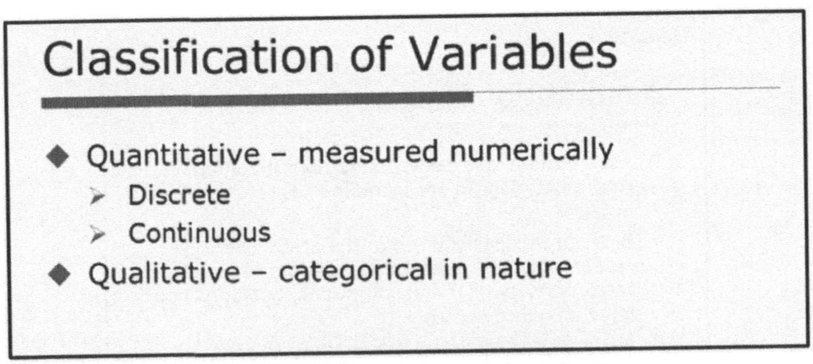

Fig. 12.19: Classification of variables

(**Source:** based on review of literature)

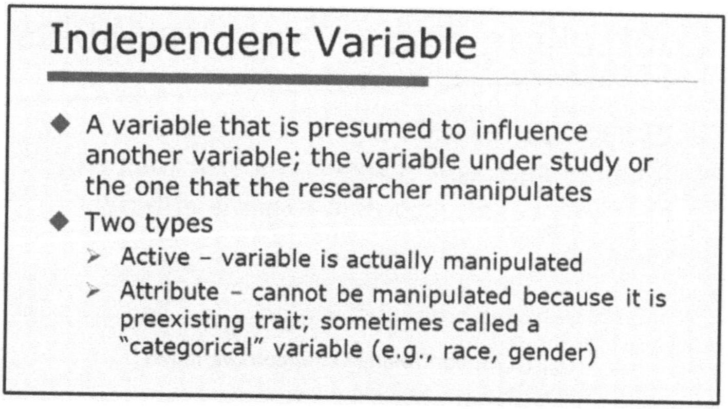

Fig. 12.20: Independent Variable

(**Source:** based on review of literature)

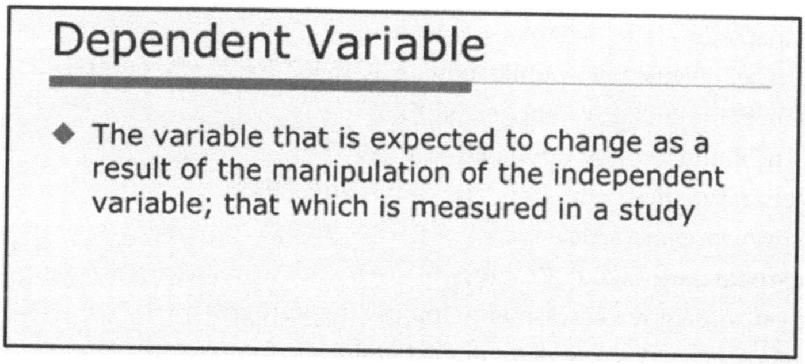

Fig. 12.21: Dependent Variable

(**Source:** based on review of literature)

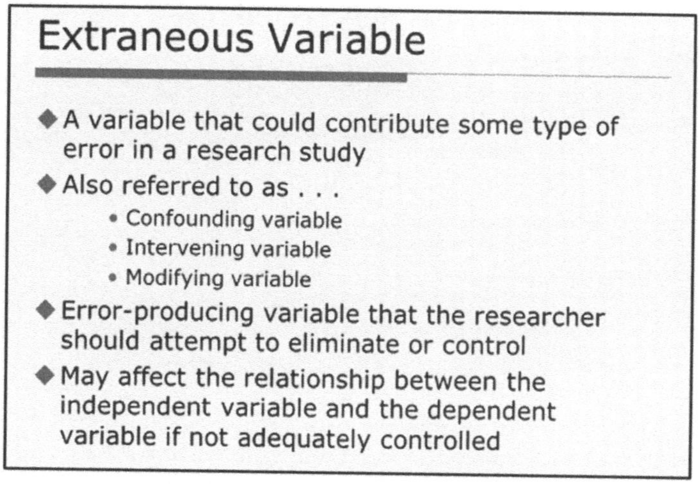

Fig. 12.22: Extraneous variable

(**Source:** based on review of literature)

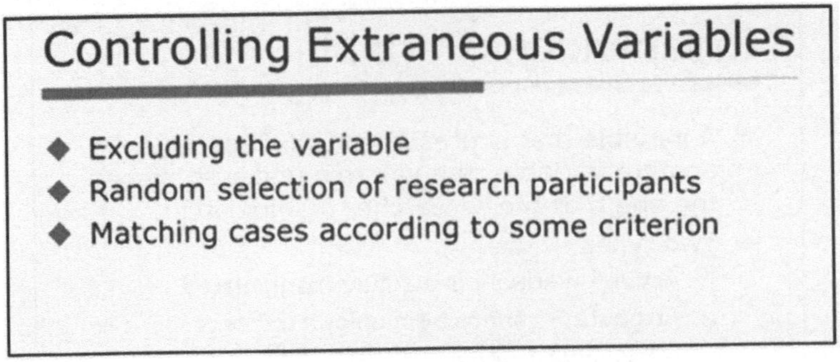

Fig. 12.23: Controlling Extraneous Variables

(**Source:** based on review of literature)

SUGGESTED READING

https://www.frontiersin.org › articles

https://www.nap.edu › read › chapter

https://www.researchgate.net › publication › 329316947_Research_progress...

https://www.ncbi.nlm.nih.gov › books › NBK26378

https://www.ncbi.nlm.nih.gov › pubmed

https://onlinelibrary.wiley.com › doi › abs › advs.201700032

https://link.springer.com › article

https://en.wikipedia.org › wiki › Progress

https://ccmc.gsfc.nasa.gov › assessment › topics › trackprogress

https://www.bristol.ac.uk › research › impact › educational-progress

Index